W9-DEM-130

CHRISTIAN SCIENCE
AND THE
MYTH OF MATTER

CHRISTIAN SCIENCE

and the

MYTH
OF
MATTER

ANN BEALS

The Bookmark
Santa Clarita, California

Beals, Ann.
    Christian Science and the myth of matter / by Ann
Beals.
    p.cm.
    Includes bibliographical references.
    LCCN 2004103989
    ISBN 0-930227-66-2

    1. Christian Science. 2. Religion and science.
    3. Cosmology. 4. Spiritual healing. I. Title.

BX6943.B432004   289.5
                    QBI04-700281

ALSO BY THE AUTHOR
The Spiritual Dimension
An Introduction to Christian Science
The Christian Science Treatment: The Prayer that Heals
Scientific Prayer
Animal Magnetism
The Prayer of Affirmation and Denial
The Law of Love
The Secret Place
Mental Malpractice
Chrsitian Science and the Threat of Mind Control

Published by
The Bookmark
Post Office Box 801143
Santa Clarita, California 91380

CONTENTS

INTRODUCTION

In the latter part of the nineteenth century something incredibly new and different was introduced into world consciousness — the scientific explanation of Christ Jesus' healing works. It appeared gently, unannounced, in a book entitled *Science and Health* by Mary Baker Eddy. By the turn of the century, Christian Science had become a worldwide movement due solely to the healing effects that this book had on those who read it. For a brief time a brilliant light was shining in the darkness and despair of humanity. Christian Science was sweeping through the world healing the sick, reforming the sinner, and bringing hope and enlightenment to those receptive to its revolutionary ideas.

This light first came into my life when I was not yet a year old. I had a severe illness that the doctors could neither diagnose nor cure. I was in a coma when my mother called a Christian Science practitioner to pray for me, and I was healed within days. This brought my family into Christian Science.

During the 1930s and 1940s when I was growing up, the Church was at the height of its prosperity, and phenomenal healing work was taking place. Many times my family turned to this same practitioner for help and healing, and we had outstanding healings through her prayerful work. My own healings gave me an unwavering faith in the power of prayer based on this Science.

After I was married with a family of my own, my faith became one of love for Christian Science because I found it to be the single most fascinating subject I had ever known. As I studied it, I had many healings for my family and myself.

I also became an active member of the Christian Science organization, serving a local church in many capacities. Soon after joining the Church, I sensed that the light that had burned so brightly and blessed so many was beginning to grow dim. Having known the Church during its most prosperous times, I could see that it was changing.

I was aware that early Christianity, along with its healing works, had gradually declined until only the faint shadow of its true teachings remained. As the decline in my own Church continued, I knew, as did others, what was being lost. I felt that it was happening because most Christian Scientists understood very little of this monumental discovery. They served the Church and depended on practitioners for healing. Those practitioners close to Mrs. Eddy's time had an understanding of this discovery that made great healers of them, but as they left us, so did the healing works that won so many to Christian Science.

I felt there had to be an answer to this impending crisis in the Church. I often wondered: What did Christ Jesus and Mrs. Eddy *know* that they could heal as they did? It had to be more than a blind faith in God, for they taught others how to heal, which meant that their healing power had to come from some form of intelligence that could be passed on from generation to generation. I asked myself many questions, and foremost among them was the one: How is it that there is no matter? Throughout her writings Mrs. Eddy states that there is no matter, yet I seemed to live in a body and a universe that depended on matter for its very existence.

I turned to the Bible and Mrs. Eddy's writings for answers to my questions, for I was deeply disturbed over the possible loss of Christian Science to this age.

At the time when I began this study, *The Saturday Evening Post* ran a series of articles entitled "Adventures of the Mind." Some of the articles were by prominent scientists in physics, astronomy and biology. I was amazed to learn that they had not yet found a final material cause for the universe. I had assumed that such a cause had long been established, but not so! The more the scientists probed into the atom, the more they learned about the universe and life, the more elusive a final cause became. Instead, there was growing evidence of a nonmaterial dimension in the universe.

I sensed in this an opening, a narrow path, that could connect the natural sciences with Christian Science in such a way that it proved Christian Science to be an advanced scientific discovery, destined to become the door to a new age. As I read books on all the main sciences, I found that there were many unknowns still present. When I came to Einstein's work, I realized that he had proven mathematically what Mrs. Eddy had discerned through revelation — there is no solid matter as we think of it. While I understood very little about the Theory of Relativity, I did know that what Mrs. Eddy had written on the unreality of matter had been proven by $E=mc_2$. The "solid forms" we live in are actually empty space and charges of energy.

At this point I began to have two images of the universe — one material, which seemed very real, and one spiritual, which seemed rather vague and theoretical. Again and again I tried to reconcile the two. Then late one night my answer came. As I stood looking at the moon while struggling with the question of two opposite concepts of the universe, the moon suddenly took on another dimension. It was as though I could look through it and discern a spiritual cause underlying it. The moon no longer appeared to be a heavy material object held in place by the mindless forces of gravity. It was almost transparent — an ethereal creation, a weightless form. I began to see it as a spiritual reality. The atoms in it were the manifestation of the thought-forces of the one Mind, and not the mindless forces of matter. The answer to my question was simple — the forces creating and governing the universe are not the mindless forces of matter, but the spiritual forces of Mind, God, hidden in a realm beyond the senses.

With that fleeting glimpse into reality, I began to see through the veil of matter. I realized that there are not two universes — one material and one spiritual. There is only one — the spiritual universe imaged forth by an infinite Mind that we, in our darkened minds, interpret as material.

I could see a way of merging the objective physical world with the subjective spiritual forces of Mind, and out of this came my first effort to present Christian Science as a scientific discovery: a book entitled *The Spiritual Dimension*.

Since the publication of this first book, the natural sciences have moved even closer to acknowledging a spiritual cause beneath the universe and man. And my own concept of reality has developed to the place where I can discern more clearly the connection between the physical realm as effect and the spiritual realm as cause.

In this book I begin where the natural sciences are today. Remarks by some of the most visionary thinkers show that the trend of science is moving towards the recognition of God as the ultimate cause of all things real. I relate Christian Science to this trend and explain its vital role as the key to this unseen realm of Mind. The conclusions of the scientists have come through their discoveries, and mine have come through prayer and revelation.

My solid world remains, but I see it differently. I have lost my fear of many material so-called laws and conditions. Understanding to some degree the unreality of matter and evil has freed me of many earthly weights. It has given me the inner strength to face and overcome challenges that seemed insurmountable. The spiritual nature of reality has grown clearer to me, and brought about many healings.

I have not tried to cover so vast a subject as Christian Science in this book. I discuss only the simple but fundamental fact that all is Mind — there is no matter, I show how this is now a logical idea, and how it can begin to replace the wrong image of a material universe with a transcending image of a spiritual one.

Hopefully this book will help renew the world's interest in Christian Science and prevent it from languishing in the depths of world consciousness while the stormy surface of events continues to carry us into a future that is not very promising.

As the natural scientists continue to recognize a thinking cause in the universe, Christian Scientists are coming to see Mrs. Eddy's revelation in a new light. They are outgrowing their dedication to a religious organization and recognizing this Science as a universal study of divine metalphysics.

With the natural scientists pressing ever deeper into the spiritual dimension and Christian Scientists moving forward into the advanced metaphysics that Mrs. Eddy has given them, the time seems right for creating a well-defined path between the cutting edge of the sciences and elementary Christian Science. I hope this book will help to do this.

Ann Beals
2004

A NEW VISION

In the beginning was the Word, and the Word was with God, and the Word was God. . . . All things were made by him; and without him was not anything made that was made.

JOHN 1:1

The universe, like man, is to be interpreted by Science from its divine Principle, God, and then it can be understood; but when explained on the basis of physical sense and represented as subject to growth, maturity, and decay, the universe, like man, is, and must continue to be, an enigma.

MARY BAKER EDDY

Unless the vast amounts of scientific data and conclusions drawn by atheistic as well as devout scientists are in extreme error, our universe had a metaphysical beginning. The existence — if the word existence applies to that which precedes our universe — of the eternal metaphysical is a scientific reality. . . . What all these conjectures have in common is that something, or more accurately stated some non-thing, an eternal whatever, predates our universe. This whatever-it-is has no bodily parts, is totally nonmaterial, is eternal, and though being absolutely nothing physically has the infinite potential to produce vast universes.

GERALD SCHROEDER

Chapter I

A NEW VISION

SINCE TIME BEGAN the mist of matter has blinded man to the true cause of the universe and to his own relationship to God. In these "latter days" now enveloping civilization, this mist has grown so thick as to leave only the dim shadows of the Divine to guide and comfort us. Overwhelming problems cause us to cry out for a vision that transcends the scientific age and provides an answer to the needs that science alone cannot give us, a vision that lifts us above the confusion, conflict and cares of the world. For this we will need a revival of our faith in God.

With the dawn of scientific thinking, the faith that ushered in the Scientific Age began to disappear. When Copernicus discovered that the earth revolved around the sun, he freed Christianity of false theology and medieval superstition, but he drained the heavens of the presence of God and displaced man as the center of his universe. Newtonian physics led to a mechanistic philosophy, in which the universe seemed to be a giant clock with little need for a God to keep it running. Darwin's "survival of the fittest" brought an even greater loss of faith. With twentieth century physics came the theory that mindless forces created the heavens and the earth through chance and probability. The universe became a godless juggernaut unconscious of man's presence and indifferent to his suffering.

As scientific technology increases the power for good, it also seems to increase the power for evil. We now foresee a future of never-ending battles between good and evil, as well as one of world-threatening catastrophes, terrorism, plagues, famine, "invasion by aliens," and "intergalactic wars." Include the growing practice of mind control and witchcraft, and the future seems dark indeed. Because of a purely material concept of the universe and the sophisticated use of modern mesmerism, our minds have been drained of the spirituality of earlier periods. The constant education in the reality of matter and the power of evil has brought a wilderness experience in which God seems all but nonexistent.

It was once believed that the sciences would bring about Utopia, but this is not happening. Instead, the media daily pours forth a steady stream of information with emphasis on the most materialistic and humanistic aspects of life. This daily diet of disturbing news darkens and materializes the mind, hardens the heart, and silences the inner voice through which God reaches us.

Unfortunately, the media is not reporting the great good that is taking place. There is beginning to shine through the heavy mist of materialism a spiritual light "greatly to be desired." The sciences have opened the way for a revelation that indicates a very different plan for the future. The scientific path is leading us back to God, and God has already provided the revelation destined to take us into a new dimension of the mind.

There is gradually unfolding in the scientific community the possibility that there is much more to the universe than material cause and effect. Chance and probability are not enough to explain the discoveries being made, and it now appears that "something more" must be originating and sustaining creation — a mysterious intangible cause of a mental or spiritual nature. After years of denying the existence of God, scientists are now finding creation so complex and profound that only a supreme intelligence could have created it. All roads are leading to an infinite Mind as the only logical explanation for the discoveries being made.

Fortunately, the vision that accurately defines this unknown realm is already present and patiently waiting to be recognized. While the surface of our world may be dark and stormy, beneath its churning surface is a revelation that is due to emerge and bring us safely through the storm. This vision is the foundation to the next logical step in the evolution of civilization.

Matter, believed to be solid substance, has disappeared from the universe. In fact, we find that it has never existed. Man has always considered matter to be the medium he lives in and the basis of all that he knows. But we now know that it has no more solidity than a thought or a feeling. Although what we know as matter has been proven to be pure energy, still the earth and man remain as tangible entities, and we must now find a new way to explain them. In Revelation John wrote, "I saw a new heaven and a new earth: for the first heaven and the first earth were passed away; and there was no more sea," indicating that the material heaven and earth are destined to be replaced by one based on spiritual cause and effect. Over the past thousand years, the focal point of men's thinking has shifted from a medieval belief in the supernatural to modern scientific knowledge. We now have to shift from physics to metaphysics, transcend our present scientific views and replace them with a knowledge of this unexplored dimension.

Because of the mental and spiritual nature of this hidden realm, a vision defining it would be very different from present scientific knowledge. It would be one that transforms the inner self. If it were merely an extension of what we already know — a mental blueprint of a material universe — it would not present a way out of the troubled-ridden life that plagues us all today. A true definition of the intangible dimension will need to go far beyond our present sense of reality and penetrate deep into the unknown. Such enlightenment is destined to renovate the mind and heart and soul, and free man of the materialism that now imprisons him. It is so different from the present concept of all things, that we cannot relate to it unless we accept the fact that our most fundamental concepts are destined to be replaced by a transcending viewpoint of reality.

Such a renovation of world consciousness will be the work of centuries, but the end result will be even more spectacular than the changes that have come about as science replaced the false theology and superstitions of the Dark Age. Those who accept this vision can begin now to replace the present primitive and basically erroneous image of the universe for a "new heaven and a new earth."

The Light Shining in the Darkness

The revelation that is the key to the spiritual realm of Mind first appeared over one hundred years ago. It was the year 1875. Natural scientists were proclaiming the universe to be as predictable as clockwork with little left to be discovered. With Darwin's *Origin of the Species*, man himself became the result of natural causes. The mechanistic philosophy was accepted without question because it had been proven scientifically.

At a time when this philosophy was entrenched in the minds of the general public, Mary Baker Eddy published the first edition of *Science and Health with Key to the Scriptures*. For many years she had been searching for the scientific laws underlying Christ Jesus' healing works. In 1866 an accident, expected to be fatal, caused her to turn once more to the Bible for help. As she prayed, her years of searching were rewarded. The spiritual laws underlying the miracles of the Bible were revealed to her. At that moment she was completely healed.

Mrs. Eddy soon found that she could heal the sick, the blind, the crippled, and the deaf and dumb through prayer alone. Moreover, when she found willing students, she was able to teach her revelation to them, and they could also heal themselves and others through prayer. As she realized the magnitude of her discovery, she published it in a book and gave it to the world.

Science and Health was destined to go through many revisions before it reached its final edition in 1910, but the publication of the first edition in 1875 marked the beginning of a new age. Long before the advent of the twentieth century physics, Mrs. Eddy wrote in this first edition, "Matter being unintelligent, there is no material law governing man and the universe." (p. 43)

"Matter is neither Intelligence, nor a creator." (p. 77)

"Spirit is Intelligence, whereas the basis of matter is belief; the former is science, the latter mesmerism." (p. 111)

"Materiality must and will go out, though it be slowly; *the spiritual era advances when physical effects will no longer be attributed to physical causes, but discerned in their final spiritual Cause.*" [Emphasis supplied.] (p. 414)

In 1910, in the last edition of the textbook, Mrs. Eddy wrote, "There is no life, truth, intelligence, nor substance in matter. All is infinite Mind and its infinite manifestation, for God is All-in-all." (p. 468)

Although Christian Science was first considered to be a religious movement, Mrs. Eddy knew it was far more than a new religion, or another method for treating sickness and disease. Christian Science introduces a transcending vision that accurately defines the structure and content of the spiritual realm that lies beyond the senses.

At a time when a materialistic philosophy dominated the scientific world, Mrs. Eddy wrote brilliantly and with great foresight about the mental and spiritual nature of creation. She succeeded in resolving the age-old conflict between science and religion, defining scientifically the spiritual cause of all things.

Mrs. Eddy presented concepts that are only now being universally considered. She defined God as the one cause and creator, and the spiritual nature of man and the universe as the effects of this one spiritual cause. She declared that there is no matter, and that evil has no power or reality beyond what the human mind gives it. She recognized sickness, disease and aging to be caused by mental and emotional disturbance. She discovered the spiritual and scientific laws underlying Christ Jesus' healing works and established a form of prayer that put spiritual healing on a scientific basis. She uncovered the lethal effect of malicious mental malpractice, witchcraft, and secret hypnosis, and showed how prayer can protect the mind from all forms of mental influence and control. She proved that the power of drugs to heal is only in proportion to one's faith in them. Above all else, her writings accurately define in depth the unseen realm now coming to light.

When Christian Science first appeared, it was so in advance of the times that it took the form of a new religion. Within Mrs. Eddy's lifetime it was widely known throughout the United States and in many foreign lands because of the healing works that came from the study of her writings — healings that equaled those of early Christianity. Many who studied Christian Science and practiced it, found they could heal sickness, disease, accidents, adversity, lack and discord through prayer alone.

For a brief period the healing works of early Christianity were again taking place throughout the world. A heavenly glow of deep spirituality shone in the darkness, bringing inspiration, hope and regeneration to thousands. After Mrs. Eddy left us, the light began to dim. Christian Science was a discovery so in advance of the time that it had little relation to the twentieth century.

It might have faded away entirely except for the fact that many who studied it continued to find healing and spiritual enlightenment. Christian Science literature that has accumulated over the past century includes thousands upon thousands of testimonies of healing, proving that in this spiritual realm there lives a healing force that has yet to be recognized by the sciences. Through their healing works, Christian Scientists have been and still are drawing upon the vast spiritual power latent in this intangible realm. Such healing works are evidence of the beneficial effect that this discovery has on the lives of those who understand it.

Venturing beyond Science and Technology

It is hard to imagine the impact that the discovery of this new dimension will have on the world. While science and technology have completely transformed our lives, the darkness in the heart and soul of humanity is still very evident. Although the scientific age has enlightened the mind, it has not eliminated man's inhumanity to man, healed mental and physical illness, overcome poverty, injustice and inequality, and put an end to war, terrorism and crime. It is becoming increasingly obvious that there are sickness-producing mental and emotional states of mind that medical science and technology are unable to reach. We will find solutions to these problems as we understand how to draw on the healing power found in this spiritual realm. And at this time we face this hidden realm without knowing what it is or what it does.

Why has science and technology failed to free us of moral, emotional, and physical illness? Because the cause or source of sickness and disease is in the mental realm where we have embedded in consciousness the concrete conviction that man and the universe are forms of matter, governed by material laws. Matter and evil seem more real to us than God. Challenges continue because this material image in the innermost thoughts objectifies itself in a material life. We assume that this material concept is not only the right one, but the *only* one.

This conviction is ingrained within us because *it has been proven scientifically*. Until the last part of the twentieth century, it appeared to be so logically conceived and so obviously right that it was accepted as fact. If the material viewpoint were indeed true and there was no alternative to it, the possibility of ever escaping sickness, disease and adversity would seem without hope.

However, we are learning that this material image is not the only one. *In fact, it is not even the right one.* Christian Science presents a transcending vision of man and the universe destined to replace the false material image. Through an understanding of this spiritual realm, we will discover that it holds the answers to problems that science and technology cannot solve.

As the Scientific Age has progressed, we have at each stage *encountered the unexpected*. Copernicus found that the earth is not the center of the universe. Galileo discovered that the heavens are not static. Newton proved that creation is not the work of supernatural forces. Einstein gave us the equation that turned seemingly solid mass into forms of energy. And now, once again, we are encountering the unexpected — that the universe and man are not the effect of material forces, but of a supreme intelligence inhabiting a dimension beyond the senses; and latent in this hidden realm is an unexpected healing power of such depth and scope that no human need is beyond its help.

If the healing works of early Christianity are any indication of the nature of this hidden realm, then it is a Mind so pure in its goodness, harmony and perfection that our present mentality bears little resemblance to it. Yet the ignorant and fearful minds of the Dark Ages gradually accepted the scientific nature of the universe. Even so, we can come to understand and be blessed by the coming enlightenment regarding God's relationship to His universe and man.

In this new millennium, the spiritual nature of man and the universe will slowly emerge as a scientific fact, revealing the Truth that men through the ages have so earnestly sought. The Scientific Age will fade into history as this realm beyond the senses becomes the new frontier of knowledge because its healing power is so desperately needed.

Presently we face this hidden realm with a mind fairly drained of the deep faith and spiritual love needed to enter it; but we will revive these Christ-like qualities when we understand the blessings that come from knowing and obeying the moral and spiritual laws of the universe. Through an inner renovation of our hearts and minds — one that spiritualizes consciousness — we will escape the discord and suffering of mortal life. Our present belief in the reality and power of matter images forth a mortal life of sin, disease, and death, but as we gain an understanding of man and the universe as the creation of God, good, our minds will image forth a life of health, happiness, and affluence.

Those who can read the signs of the times can see that we are entering a new era — one that will transform world consciousness and bring about even greater change than that which the scientific age has brought us.

This unseen realm is being gradually acknowledged by psychology, religion, and medicine, as well as science, but science has arrived at the edge of it through discoveries that *prove* the presence of God in the universe. Many books by scientists and scientific investigators now acknowledge the presence of an intelligent cause in the universe.

In the *Science of God*, Gerald Schroeder writes of this possibility: "As a scientist trained at the Massachusetts Institute of Technology, I was convinced I had the information to exclude Him — or is it Her? — from the grand scheme of life. But with each step forward in the unfolding mystery of the cosmos, a subtle yet pervading ingenuity, a contingency kept shining through, a contingency that joins all aspects of existence into a coherent unity. While this coherence does not prove the existence of a Designer, it does call out for interpretation."

Kitty Ferguson says it even more directly in her book, *The Fire in the Equations*: "Suppose one believes in God not as the embodiment of the laws of physics, but as the *source* of them, a God behind and beyond the laws — or, even more fundamental than that, the creator of a context in which such laws would inevitably arise and make a universe. This God wouldn't be a person. A Mind perhaps, but we shouldn't expect to have a word or concept that fits."

We must now renew and deepen our faith in God and come to understand this invisible realm scientifically, if we are to find answers to those problems that science and technology cannot resolve.

How does this Mind create all things? How did the universe and man, being so visible and solid, come from a wholly non-material source? How can we learn what is in this spiritual realm? How can we exchange the material view for one that relates intelligently to God? These are questions we are going to consider in the coming chapters.

THE DECLINE OF THE SCIENTIFIC AGE

In the beginning God created the heaven and the earth.

GENESIS 1:1

Christian Science translates Mind, God, to mortals. It is the infinite calculus defining the line, place, space, and fourth dimension of Spirit. . . . . Science, understood, translates matter into Mind, rejects all other theories of causation, restores the spiritual and original meaning of Scriptures, and explains the teaching and life of our Lord.

MARY BAKER EDDY

The stream of knowledge is heading towards a non-mechanical reality; the universe begins to look more like a great thought than a great machine. . . . The old dualism of mind and matter is disappearing and matter is resolving into a creation of the mind.

SIR JAMES JEANS

Chapter II

THE DECLINE OF THE SCIENTIFIC AGE

FUTURE GENERATIONS will look back on the dawn of the Spiritual Age as the inevitable outcome of the Scientific Age, which was needed to bring about a universal acknowledgment of the spiritual realm of Mind and the Science that explains it.

We today do not have the privilege of such hindsight. We live on the cutting edge of this renovation of human consciousness. The simple world of yesterday is gone. The mental foundations it rested upon have crumbled away, and we have entered a transitional period that is in some ways comparable to the wilderness experience of the Children of Israel. During their forty years in the desert, they learned to adjust to an unfamiliar state of mind and a new way of life. And we are faced with the same challenge.

We have no choice but to go forward as the truth, shining in the darkness of mortal thought, lights the way. Although we may resist new ideas that challenge our most ingrained beliefs, still the acceptance of them will come as the world learns of the healing power latent in this spiritual realm.

Science and religion have been considered opposites over the centuries, but time is destined to unite them into one transcending form of metaphysics. Both are essential to an understanding of the qualities, laws, and structure of the spiritual dimension, but there must be a logical path connecting the two. The visible must fuse with the invisible in such a way that there is an intelligent explanation of their relationship.

Faith that we can understand the spiritual realm has its roots in the beginning of modern science. At the close of the Dark Ages, this faith in the presence of God permeated Western civiliza-

15

tion. In small village churches and towering cathedrals, the Gospel of Love was taught and lived by millions. The Christian way of life was so deep and strong that it united the whole of Europe in a religion that not only taught that God is Love, but that He is also a rational Being. The more visionary minds of the time began to reason that a rational God would create a rational universe. By understanding His handiwork, they hoped to understand the Creator, and so a strong faith in a rational God gave birth to the Scientific Age. But this spiritual foundation began to fade when the universe appeared to be nothing more than a perfectly tuned watch and the mechanistic philosophy prevailed. In time this viewpoint was replaced with Einstein's theory of relativity and quantum mechanics.

Twentieth century physics went even further and suggested that there is no absolute truth, that all things are relative, and creation is the product of chance and probability. This resulted in an atheistic basis to modern philosophies. Each scientific discovery seemed to reinforced this negative view, creating an ever-greater estrangement between man and his Creator. It was as though the goal of science has been to prove there is no God — all is material cause and effect. Because science could prove its claims, it appeared that science and religion were irreconcilable, and science seemed destined to replace religion.

Instead, now, there has come about a disenchantment with science, for it has failed to solve humanity's woes. At the same time there is unfolding new evidence that God is the true cause of all things. The presence of God in the universe is returning *through the avenues of science*. The scientific community is beginning once again to recognize God as the primal cause and creator.

This rather recent development is the result of the sophisticated technology that enabled scientists in their special fields to study in great detail the atom and the cell, and to explore the farthest reaches of outer space. After decades of working independently of each other, scientists began to assemble the results of their various discoveries into one vast picture. They pooled many seemingly unrelated facts into one overall picture, and once again they were confronted with the unexpected: *the universe is far too intelligent and complex to be the result of non-intelligent forces and mindless atoms.* The construction of the universe is so profound and complete that it must be the effect of a supreme intelligence. The universe is not only rational, but it has plan and purpose, design and unity, order and direction to such a degree that "something more" must underlie it, a hidden cause that science and technology cannot fathom. The universe could only be the product of an infinite Mind. As this becomes increasingly obvious, we come full circle back to God as the Creator. God is not dead, but living in an invisible, intangible dimension that lies beyond the senses, and neither science nor religion alone can reveal the structure and content of it. Faith in God will not be enough to make full use of the healing power in this realm, and the sciences alone cannot pry open its secrets. This dimension must be spiritually defined and scientifically understood if we are to draw freely on its healing potential. We are no longer seeking to understand the works of God, but God Himself.

Patrick Glynn writes in *God: The Evidence*: "Such is the great surprise as the twentieth century turns into the twenty-first: The very logic of human inquiry is compelling a rediscovery of the realm of spirit, of God and the soul. . . . A generation and more ago, secular thinkers were filled with faith in reason and convinced that the scientific worldview was destined to replace the religious one. Modern thinkers predicted the 'disenchantment of the world' — the disappearance of God from the human horizon. What our century has experienced instead is disenchantment with reason, the collapse of the Enlightenment's secular and rational faith. Perhaps not entirely so coincidentally, God is reemerging in Western intellectual life at the very moment when reason seems to have hit the end of the road."

Michael J. Denton explains this recent development in his book *Nature's Destiny*: "Four centuries after the scientific revolution apparently destroyed irretrievably man's special place in the universe, banished Aristotle, and rendered teleological speculation obsolete, the relentless stream of discovery has turned dramatically in favor of teleology and design, and the doctrine of the microcosm is reborn. . . . Science, which has been for centuries the great ally of atheism and skepticism, has come at last, in these final days of the second millennium, to what Newton and many of its early advocates had so fervently wished — the defender of the anthropocentric faith."

The Decline of the Scientific Age

The growing recognition of God as a presence in the universe has come through the discoveries of science, and the search for the ultimate cause is moving into the realm of metaphysics. With this unforeseen development has come a reassessment of the future of the natural sciences. There are several reasons for questioning their future.

First: The great Scientific Age seems to be drawing to a close because research into the minutest forms of matter and the farthest reaches of outer space seem all but exhausted. In a sense we have pressed through the atom and reduced the universe to nonmaterial waves of energy. There seem to be no more great mysteries left in the physical universe for the sciences to explore. Cosmologists are now trying to find an equation that unifies gravity, electromagnetism, and the weak and strong nuclear forces. It is known as the Theory of Everything. But this equation has yet to be formulated, and when it does appear, it will not be enough to resolve the challenges that are beyond the reach of science and technology. As for the immediate future, the development of technology and the application of scientific findings seem almost limitless, but the scientific discoveries that changed our image of the universe and gave birth to the modern world appear a thing of the past. The realm of metaphysics has become the new frontier.

Second: The sciences have never found a final material cause for life and evolution, or for the energy that makes up the universe. In searching for a final cause, they have pressed through the physical realm into an intangible dimension without a clue as to the real origin of energy and life. No material cause for either has been defined by mathematical equation or scientific experiment, and no clue as to the nature of this new dimension seems forthcoming through scientific methods. The origin or cause of all things remains a mystery.

In *The Big Bang Never Happened*, Eric J. Lerner writes: " . . . our universe appears to have a very significant amount of energy tied up in existing matter. Where did THAT energy come from? Is there more? . . . We simply DO NOT KNOW where the energy in matter derives from, and we do not know whether and under what circumstances it can be captured or released." He also adds, "Since nowhere do we see something emerge from nothing, we have no reason to think this occurred in the distant past. Instead plasma cosmology assumes that, because we now see an evolving, changing universe, the universe has always existed and always evolved, and will exist and evolve for an infinite time to come."

Edwin Turner in *The Light at the Edge of the Universe* writes: "We more or less don't know how *anything* forms — dust, stars, galaxies — anything."

In *The Universe: Plan or Accident*, Robert E. D. Clark concludes that it is "impossible, or at least extremely difficult, to avoid the conclusion that the plan of the universe was due to a Mind behind it — a Mind separate from nature but able to act upon nature from without."

And in *The Hidden Face of God*, Gerald Schroeder writes: "Wisdom is the fundamental building block of the universe, and it is inherent in all parts. In the processes of life it finds its most complex revelation. Wisdom, information, an idea, is the link between the metaphysical Creator and the physical creation. It is the hidden face of God."

19

Third: The most unexpected result of all scientific work is the discovery that everywhere, and in everything, there is design and plan. The complexity of all things — from the infinitesimal to infinity — appears to be the work of a Mind so vast and so superior to our own mind that our feeble efforts to define it are hopelessly inadequate. Chance and probability could never account for the order, plan, design and purpose of creation as we are coming to see it. There must be an intelligent cause behind each phase of the evolutionary process.

In *God: The Evidence*, Mr. Glynn writes: "Modern thinkers assumed that science would reveal the universe to be ever more random and mechanical; instead, it has discovered unexpected new layers of intricate order that bespeak an almost unimaginably vast master plan."

John Horgan writes in *The End of Science*: "The more clearly we can see the universe in all its glorious detail, the more difficult it will be for us to explain with a simple theory how it came to be that way."

Fourth: It appears that man is not a small speck of living dust adrift in a giant mindless juggernaut. When all of the facts are in, they indicate that the universe has been carefully designed and created as a home for him. Man is once again the center of God's creation, the purpose in all that He does. This has led to the *anthropic principle* — meaning that the universe was created for man. Moreover, this is not just a religious belief, but a principle deduced from scientific facts.

Brandon Carter in 1974 was the first to call it the anthropic principle. And of this Mr. Glynn writes in *God: The Evidence*: "The anthropic principle marked an important turning point in the history of science: the first time a scientific discovery seemed to take us toward, rather than away from, the idea that there is a God. For hundreds of years science had been whittling away at the proposition that the universe was created or designed. Suddenly scientists came upon a series of facts that seemed to point toward precisely such a conclusion — the universe is the product of intelligence and aim, that in the absence of an intelligent organization of a thousand details vast and small, we would not exist. . . . Today the concrete data points strongly in the direction of the God hypothesis. It is the simplest and most obvious solution to the anthropic puzzle."

A New Dimension

Because there is a limit to what can be observed by the five senses, the age of science appears to be slowly declining. Although this age has not provided solutions to many of humanity's problems, the sciences have not left us without hope of finding answers to them. The fading Scientific Age has opened up a new dimension to the universe that holds solutions to problems that are beyond science and technology. The theory of "something more" is the beginning of a transformation of world consciousness in which a spiritual view of reality is destined to replace the material view.

When Einstein discovered that $E=mc_2$ he proved that mass is actually energy in a crystallized or frozen form. Thus, there is no solid matter as we think of it. Yet the world goes on believing in matter and suffering from the effects of this illusion. In order to be free of this illusion of matter and the discordant life it produces, there must be a transcending vision to replace it.

Far more is needed than an extension of the material viewpoint or a refinement of any philosophy based on matter as real. The veil of matter has darkened the human mind since the earliest records of civilization; but *matter is a myth*, a form of mesmerism to be outgrown as we evolve into a metaphysical age.

How can we begin to awaken from this dream of life and intelligence in matter? The answer is simple — *we can add a spiritual dimension to the universe and man*. This is possible because science has never found a definite material cause for creation, because matter itself as nonmaterial as a thought or a feeling. There-

21

fore, in view of the nonmaterial nature of creation, it is possible to add a nonmaterial dimension to it as the real cause. By adding a spiritual dimension to creation, we are not changing the universe; we are learning to interpret it with more accuracy.

When scientists discovered that the universe is governed by scientific laws, they changed our mental image of creation. This transformation was entirely subjective. It was a change of mind that brought humanity a better concept of reality.

Even so, this present challenge to dematerialize or spiritualize our mental image of the universe calls for nothing more than a change in the way we think. This subjective change will bring about a more advanced intelligence, a truer concept of reality, and the means for resolving the challenges we face. The spiritual dimension is not new. It has existed throughout eternity. We are already living in it. This dimension is the *final* source, the *main* cause and origin of all things real.

Visualizing the Spiritual Dimension

To understand what the discovery of this dimension means in relation to our present times, we can go back to the first millennium — 1000 A.D. At that time the people had a form of intelligence based on false theology and superstitious beliefs. Their lives were poor and wretched. During his lifetime, the average person did not venture more than a few miles from his birthplace.

Those people lived on the same planet we do and were governed by the same scientific laws, but they knew nothing of the scientific dimension they were living in. Even though the people lived in this dimension, they were totally *unconscious* of its existence. Their minds were dark and their lives were short and toilsome because this realm was unknown to them. Today scientific technology is the foundation of the modern world. A civilization undreamed of by the medieval mind has become a concrete reality, one that we live in with ease.

Even so, our present relation to the spiritual realm is comparable to that of the medieval mind to the scientific realm. Our world is *unconscious* of this spiritual dimension. Humanity lives in it and is governed by it, and yet is unaware of it. Because its nature is unknown, we have yet to learn how to draw upon its healing power as a means for resolving our problems.

To understand this hidden realm, we must look *through* the visible world and discern underlying it and *in addition to it*, this spiritual dimension. We can transcend the material concept of man and the universe by learning the nature of the supreme Being that inhabits this unseen realm, and creates and sustains the heavens and the earth as a home for man.

The scientific community is acknowledging more and more the presence of a universal divine Being, vaguely defined by theologians and now a proven fact by the sciences. After years of rejecting God as the supreme cause, scientists are having to acknowledge His presence because they are running out of every other possible explanation for the universe as we are coming to know it.

Asking the Right Question

Reference to God sometimes brings up the question: "But who created God?" This could be called an *improper question* for there is no way to answer it. Do we ask where did math come from? who invented music? God is a "given." We must begin with certain assumptions that are because they are. We will not learn about the spiritual dimension by asking where did God come from? or who created God? He is the premise, something we accept as true without further questioning. This provides a beginning for our emergence out of the darkness that the veil of matter has cast over our minds. The proper question should be: How can we understand God? As we understand Him, the question as to where He came from could be answered by the fact that He simply *is*.

Beginning with God as a "given," we can next define Him as a "mathematical" Mind, for the foundation of the natural sciences is based on mathematics. But God is far more than the supreme Mathematician. The human mind can be mathematical, but it is also a mind that knows much more than math. Thus, we can conclude that Mind — although it is mathematical — is also a Mind embodying a full range of spiritual qualities that will come to light as we understand this hidden realm.

We can hardly imagine the long-term planning, the gentle and careful evolution, the on-going creativity, the inexhaustible love, and supreme intelligence that God has given to creating the earth as a home for His image and likeness — man.

As we explore this hidden realm, we leave behind the myth of matter and learn to translate man and the universe as a spiritual creation coming from a spiritual cause. Just as the scientific discoveries brought to humanity a scientific world, so revelation will enable us to transcend the present belief in the reality of matter for an advanced intelligence that is expressed in a spiritually enlightened civilization.

In order to approach this realm scientifically, we should first consider some of the discoveries that have led to the revival of God as the one Supreme Cause.

ENTERING THE SPIRITUAL REALM

Behold, I create new heavens and a new earth: and the former shall not be remembered, nor come to mind

ISAIAH

Mind, supreme over all of its formations and governing them all, is the central sun of its own systems of ideas, the life and light of all its own vast creation; and man is tributary to divine Mind. The world would collapse without Mind, without the intelligence which holds the winds in its grasp.

MARY BAKER EDDY

Today . . . the physicists find themselves constantly looking over their shoulder at the theologians, who watch with intrigue as the scientists are forced to wrestle anew with an issue they thought they had put to rest a long time ago: God

PATRICK GLYNN

Chapter III

ENTERING THE SPIRITUAL REALM

THE OPENING of the new millennium brought with it the seeds of hope and healing for all mankind. Germinating in the minds of those searching for truth, watered by a return to faith in God, planted deep beneath the surface of world consciousness, they will gradually bring to fruition the "new heavens and the new earth" promised by John of Patmos.

We know now that the universe is far too rational to be the result of non-intelligent forces and mindless atoms. Hidden in a mysterious realm beyond the senses is an intelligent Cause infinitely greater than anything we can imagine. *The scientific recognition of the realm of God, Mind, is one of the most significant events in the history of civilization.* The full impact of this discovery will be apparent when the healing power in this realm dawns on the world in general. We will come to understand this Mind as we fuse together Christianity and science into one final system of ideas.

This unseen dimension is far more complex than the scientific dimension. The intelligence, wisdom, and creativity in it is God-like, making this coming age one of *divine metaphysics.*

Entrance into this spiritual realm will bring to the modern mind a new form of intelligence, just as the past millennium changed the medieval mind into a science-saturated mind. Slowly humanity will develop a spiritually enlightened mentality that uses the healing power latent in this hidden realm as freely and knowledgeably as we use scientific technology today.

Already many scientists, philosophers, and journalists are

acknowledging that something new and different has come to light. Mr. Schroeder writes in his book, *The Hidden Face of God*, "Atheist, agnostic, skeptic, and 'believer' all share the understanding that some metaphysical non-thing, metaphysical in the sense of being alone or outside of the physical, must have preceded our universe or have our universe imbedded in it. That much is a certainty."

And again he writes, "Is God immanent? I would not attempt to prove a case for divine direction. But there is a certainty: twentieth century physics has opened the door, and opened it wide, for that interpretation. . . . Our universe, tuned so accurately for the needs of intelligent life, indeed ticks to the beat of a very skillful Watchmaker."

Defining the Spiritual Dimension

The universe is a living, evolving work in progress. The Mind that creates it is different from human thoughts and emotions. It is a distinct, independent Mind, a thinking cause, an incorporeal power and presence permeating all time and space. Its thought-forces provide a consistently rational and stable foundation to all things.

Being wholly mental, it is defined in terms of *qualities*. The natural sciences work with quantities — weight, density, strength, color, form, composition, etc. The spiritual dimension is defined by qualities — intelligence, wisdom, logic, plan, direction, purpose, creativity, design, law, order, unity. Through these qualities, Mind, working on a universal scale, creates energy, builds the universe, plans the suns and planets, originates and evolves nature and man, and does so through spiritual, not material, means.

The universe is not a hodgepodge of happenings. It is an orderly unfoldment that extends over inconceivable spans of time. Everything in it has a time, place, and purpose. Starting with the smallest visible manifestation, the hydrogen atom, it unfolds in one unbroken chain of events to the complex civilized world of today.

In considering the orderly unfoldment of the universe, many questions present themselves. Where does the directing force behind this plan originate? What creates galaxies with solar systems that sustain life? Where does life come from? What plans the intricate adaptation and interdependency of all creatures in nature? What has brought about the evolution of man and the rise of modern civilization?

In the light of what we now know about the universe, certain qualities sketch for us our first accurate insight into this hidden dimension. Most apparent are the qualities of *intelligence, unity and wholeness, plan and direction, law and order, design and creativity.*

A primary quality of Mind is *intelligence* — an infallible intelligence that creates, sustains, and governs all things from a spinning galaxy to a rose in bloom. When the rationality and workability of the whole universe is considered, a universal Mind of infinite intelligence would seem a more logical cause than nonintelligent atoms and mindless forces. This intelligence lives at the very heart of the universe as the spiritual cause of all things.

Intelligence permeates the whole of creation. The ability to create and maintain such a perfectly tuned universe would require an infallible, infinite intelligence, for nothing less could do this. Moreover, this Mind has a purpose and goal. The many laws of physics — the values of certain fundamental constants, such as the gravitational force or the electromagnetic force and their relation to each other; the restrictions placed on the size, weight, motion, density, place and purpose of all things in time and space — are more than a coincidence. The entire evolution of the heavens and the earth are directed toward one goal: that of creating and sustaining life. When the overall picture is pieced together, the universe appears to be intelligently designed to be nothing less than a home for man.

In the spiritual dimension, there are no conflicting thought-forces competing with each other. There is only one Mind expressing *wholeness* and *unity*. The atomic universe is a completely unified system throughout all time and space, with the same chemistry, the same celestial mechanics, the same gravitational and nuclear laws. The infinity we live in is one, not many. The same laws that govern the hundred billion galaxies in the heavens above, also govern the chemistry in the microscopic cell and the clouds of energy in the atoms on earth. From the infinitesimal to infinity, there is only one set of laws governing impartially and universally. They are absolute. They do not change with time, but are the same today as they were in the beginning, and ever will be.

Two more qualities found in the universe are *plan* and *direction*. The operation of the universe is not chaotic, fickle, confused, or unpredictable, but totally planned and directed by the one Mind. Each stage in the evolutionary plan follows the previous one, as galaxies, stars, planets, life and man unfold in one continuous stream of events. Nothing happens out of order. Each thing, each event, is perfectly adjusted to its time, place, and purpose in the scheme of things. This suggests a Mind that always knows what it is doing, and does it to perfection. There are no mistakes, no incompleteness, no incompetence, no disorder, lack or failure in the functioning of the universe.

Because there is one Mind, we do not sense this evolution going on around us because it is effortless, gentle, and positive. With only one Mind creating a unified universe, there would be only one power — a spiritual power that has no opposition to its activity. There is no negative force resisting Mind's expression of its ideas; only the harmonious unfoldment of its plan and purpose.

Scientists have assumed the universe would be ever more random and chaotic; instead they are finding depths of such intricate order as to suggest a master plan. From the ten thousand billion billion stars found in a hundred billion galaxies down to 0.001 centimeter of a cell, there is one set of laws. A unifying Principle runs throughout the whole of nature, which indicates that the planning and direction taking place in the spiritual dimension must be even more staggering than we can imagine.

Until recently, scientists assumed that the universe was decaying and moving towards a "heat death." But now they find that it is actually moving towards increasingly complex structures in an overall plan that is one of continuous creativity. The universe and life are not random or accidental, but pre-planned, with man as the object for which it has been so carefully orchestrated.

There is also *law* and *order* throughout creation. The divine Mind is the one Principle that governs with laws that are logical, absolute, eternal, universal, and all-powerful. These laws give order and stability to creation. God is more than the embodiment of these laws. He is the origin of them, the source behind them, the power that enforces them.

Man's divinely prepared home is not stagnant, for the universe is always in a state of change. Evolution produces a dynamic creation coming from *creativity* and *design* in the spiritual dimension. The one Mind creates with originality, beauty, harmony, and perfection. The universe is a manifestation of ideas that first originate in Mind, and are then manifested as galaxies and ladybugs, sunlight and springtime, daffodils and bubbling brooks. This orderly process suggests a creativity that never lacks for original ideas, yet its creativity is governed by law and order, plan and direction, and by the infallible intelligence of the one Mind.

In *The Universe: Plan or Accident*, Mr. Clark observes: "Design — or at least the *appearance* of design — runs like a silver thread through every main branch of science. We have seen evidences of its presence in physics, in astronomy, in chemistry and in biology. It confronts us no matter what part of nature it is that we examine — whether it is the remote nebulae, small organisms under the microscope or the atoms of chemistry. Why should we be surprised, then, to discover that wholly distinct branches have this in common, that one and all show evidences of plan or design that runs, as a unifying principle, throughout the whole domain of nature? The recognition of this design is not a quasi-scientific irrelevancy, introduced by philosophers, or theologians; it is the climax of a unifying tendency in science itself."

31

Over the centuries these qualities of God have been recognized by many religious and scientific thinkers, but there was disagreement as to whether they proved the existence of God, or whether they were due to material causes. Science, in its systematic search for truth, has long been the antithesis of religion with its worship of a Supreme Being and its faith in miracles and the supernatural. But this is no longer the case. Scientists themselves are realizing that physical causes alone could never produce a creation so complex and elaborate, so exquisite and flawless. And so we see a new image of the universe appearing on the mental horizon. God inhabits this unseen realm as the ultimate Cause. Science can no longer deny the presence of God and attribute all things to the mindless forces of matter. The acknowledgment of God as the only Creator is inevitable.

Discoveries that Prove God's Presence

The recognition of this radically new view of reality has not come easily to a scientific community that based all of its discoveries on material cause and effect. There had to be convincing proof of this realm of Mind in every scientific field if it were to be established as fact. And, indeed, there has been enough proof to bring about such an acknowledgment. The basic qualities of Mind, such as intelligence, creativity, plan, direction, unity, and design are present throughout all the scientific fields. The scientific data that established these qualities are, for the most part, too technical to be summarized in a few sentences, but those who have an understanding of them concur that something more than material cause and effect is behind the whole of creation.

While we cannot review all of these discoveries in this book, we can consider a few that give some indication of the volume of information that has brought about this stunning new development, one destined to change our image of reality.

The recognition of "something more" in the universe began when Einstein discovered the nonmaterial nature of what appears to be solid matter. The Einstein equation revealed that there are not two basic elements — mass and energy — but one: energy. Mass is congealed energy. Solid mass as we think of it, is energy in a different form. This nonmaterial state of everything we live in — our body, our world, our universe — is one of the most startling discoveries ever made.

We live in a world and a body that is 99.9999999999999 percent empty space. The remaining percent is made up of nonmaterial fields that give the impression that visible forms are solid. The fields themselves have no material essence. There is not one solid thing in the universe. All things large and small are formed of condensed energy. There is no explanation as to where this energy comes from. 'Energy' is a word used to define what we observe, but it is itself intangible. Beyond energy lies the intelligence and wisdom of a thinking cause that creates and controls all visible and invisible forms of energy. Thus we have a nonmaterial source creating a universe that is nonmaterial.

The discoveries in physics, cosmology, evolution, and biochemistry show that that the universe could never have come about through mindless forces acting on inert matter because there is simply not time enough for chance and probability to produce a universe so perfect and complete.

The universe has been created with astonishing *precision*. The mathematical foundation is so exact that it could only originate in a supreme intelligence. Planetary systems that can sustain life are possible because the structure of the universe and the laws of nature are *precisely* as they are. If the mathematical values of these laws changed by the tiniest fraction, they would produce a very different universe. Constants such as the gravitational and electromagnetic forces are so crucial that the slightest change would result in a universe that could not sustain life.

In *Equations of Eternity*, David Darling writes: " . . . the cosmos is uncannily well suited to our existence. The slightest change in any basic law or fundamental constant would preclude the development of life. Even the size of the universe and the amount of matter it contains appear to be finely tuned in order that life can spring up."

Roger Penrose, in *The Emperor's New Mind*, tells exactly "how precise the Creator's aim must have been, namely to an accuracy of one part in $10^{10^{123}}$. This is an extraordinary figure." In other words, the precision needed for the conditions and energy distribution to produce a universe that could sustain life is less than one chance in ten to the power of ten to the power of 123. That is one chance out of a billion, billion, etc. repeated more than a billion, billion times.

Michael Turner, astrophysicist at the University of Chicago and Fermilab, described the precision of the universe in this way: "The precision is as if one could throw a dart across the entire universe and hit a bull's-eye one millimeter in diameter on the other side."

If our universe were not so finely balanced, it would expand so fast that stars and planets would have no time to form, and the universe would be nothing but a mist of dust, or it would collapse before galaxies could form. The universe expands at a fixed rate between eventual collapse and eternal expansion — a fine line upon which life depends. Two opposing factors control the overall dynamics and evolution of the universe: the kinetic energy of expansion and the gravitational binding energy of matter. There is no reason why these two factors should be so perfectly balanced, but they are — a fact vital to the development of life. The growth of the universe is exactly the proper rate to allow new galaxies and stars to form. And this is only one of countless regulations, laws, and values that make it possible for life to exist.

To give a few more examples:

The distance between the stars in our galaxy is such that if the distance were much less, the orbits in our solar system would be unstable. If it were much more, the heavier elements thrown out by supernova would be so diffused that there could be no solar systems like our own.

The structure of stars is dependent on the exact ratio of electromagnetic to gravitational forces. Astrophysicist Brandon Carter has calculated that if gravity's force were to differ from what it is by only one part in 10^{-40}, stars like our sun could not form.

These few examples barely touch on the many facts that bring to light the precision necessary for our very existence. We know, for example, that the emission frequencies of light from the sun match the absorption frequencies for photosynthesis of plants on earth. Who would have supposed that such a law had been made so precise as to insure that our planet earth would be a beautiful green home for us.

Such amazing tolerances are also found in physics. Atoms have finely tuned values. The stable nuclei of the atom hinges on the precise strength of the stronger nuclear force and the electromagnetic force. A slight change in the relative strength of these two forces would cause atomic nuclei to disintegrate. If the strong nuclear force were just slightly weaker, the only element in the universe would be hydrogen. If the energy level in the oxygen nucleus were .5 percent higher, all the carbon produced in a star's core would burn immediately to oxygen and none would be left for creating a planet that supports life. If the nuclear strong force were increased by as little as 2 percent, it would prevent the formation of protons, which would mean a universe without atoms. If it decreased by 5 percent, there would be no stars.

Gravity is roughly 10^{-39} times weaker than electromagnetism. If gravity were 10^{-33} time's weaker than electromagnetism, the stars would burn a million times faster. The nuclear weak force is 10^{-28} times the strength of gravity. Had the weak force been slightly weaker, all the hydrogen in the universe would have turned to helium.

There is no explanation for gravity, since all atomic forms have no more solid substance than a thought or a feeling. Why is there weight in everything? Why does the moon orbit the earth, and why do snowflakes drift to the ground?

Radioactive atoms have a half period of 3.83 days. If we begin with a billion radioactive atoms, half will decay in 3.83 days. Then a quarter in another 3.85 days. Some will decay in a second and some in a century. How do they decide how many must decay today and how many must do so in a hundred years? Is matter in some sense aware of its environment?

These few examples of precision are selected because they are easy to understand. Many more astonishing discoveries have been made, but they would require long, detailed, technical explanations. Since the focus of this book is on the unreality of matter, these few examples seem enough to illustrate the main point — that there is "something more" than material cause and effect determining the laws governing the universe.

Plan and Design

In addition to mathematical precision, there is also the element of *design* and *plan*. Design and plan have come to light in a most astonishing way in biochemistry and evolution. When Darwin published his theory of evolution, it was assumed that life began in some warm little pond long ago and slowly evolved into the life forms we have today. It was believed that with the proper combination of chemicals, life could be created in the laboratory; but in fact, living things have systems so carefully engineered that there can be no explanation for them except to attribute them to the designing and planning of a supreme intelligence.

Biochemists have discovered that the simplest cells have been carefully designed and engineered with dozens, or even hundreds, of precisely tailored parts. In these molecular machines, the components meet each other in precise places, and align with each other in exact ways. Each cell is an exquisite mechanism that accomplishes a specific work. Because the cell's functions are totally dependent on exact interactions of the parts, we must conclude that they were created not by laws of chance and necessity, but were logically designed and planned. They were the products of intelligent creativity. The chemical life of the cell is found to be as complex as a television set or an automobile.

This discovery of the preplanned and minutely designed cell completely contradicts Darwin's conclusions as to the origin and evolution of life. It has left the scientific community without an explanation as to how life began and how it evolves. The complexity of the cell alone indicates it could not have been created by slow evolutionary processes any more than one can build a car by evolving it one part at a time. It must be put together all at once, with all the parts in place, if it is to run. Even so, a cell could not have evolved, but must have appeared from the beginning as a perfectly functioning unit. As to how the complex cell came about, the scientific community is silent.

In *Darwin's Black Box*, Michael J. Behe writes: "The result of these cumulative efforts to investigate the cell — to investigate life at the molecular level — is a loud, clear, piercing cry of '*design!*' The result is so unambiguous and so significant that it must be ranked as one of the greatest achievements in the history of science. The discovery rivals those of Newton and Einstein, Lavoisier and Schrodinger, Pasteur, and Darwin. The observation of the intelligent design of life is as momentous as the observation that the earth goes around the sun or that disease is caused by bacteria or that radiation is emitted in quanta." He adds, " . . . . we are left with no substantive defense against what feels to be a strange conclusion: that life was designed by an intelligent agent. . . . The simplicity that was once expected to be the foundation of life has proven to be a phantom; instead, systems of horrendous, irreducible complexity inhabit the cell. The resulting realization that life was designed by an intelligence is a shock to us in the twentieth century who have gotten used to thinking of life as the result of simple natural laws."

We know now that the origin of life did not take place as the result of chemicals acting and reacting in the warm little ponds of a new planet. Fossils have been found that date as far back as 3.8 billion years. It seems that living organisms appeared suddenly, as soon as the earth had cooled sufficiently and water was available. One celled organisms — bacteria and algae — appeared very early in the earth's history. For over three billion years these one-celled organisms were the only forms of life. Then some 530 million years ago life began to evolve into many forms, suggesting that there was something controlling the evolutionary process. The flow and direction of evolution is always from lower forms to higher forms of life with ever increasing intelligence, beauty, and refinement. Here again, past assumptions based on material causes must be replaced with a more metaphysical explanation of the presence of life on earth.

The carefully planned earth, with just the right elements to support life, is located at just the right distance from the sun to nurture the beginning and evolution of life, and the presence of man appears to be the purpose of such long-term planning and creativity. Thus we have the anthrophic principle, meaning that the principle and purpose behind the universe is to establish a home for man in God's likeness. Anthrophic means related to humankind. In the anthrophic principle, force, causality, space, time, and mathematical laws are just as anthropomorphic as love, hate, inspiration, intuition, intelligence, and faith. And so we see coming to light a mystifying presence that bears the name of "God."

The Universe God-sustained

Without the intelligent organization of thousands of details, we would not exist. The development of order in the galaxies and stars, life and civilization, the very lawful nature of the universe itself has to be intentional design, and this calls into question the theory that the universe began with the Big-bang. Since something cannot emerge from nothing, in the present sense of things, did this actually happen in the distant past? Did creation have such a violent beginning? Because the universe now appears to be a constantly evolving creation, it is possible that creation has always existed, and will do so eternally, for the supreme cause underlying it is "the eternal God." And what did God do before the Big-bang? Perhaps the universe has existed forever — without beginning or end — which would relate more reasonably to the idea of an eternal God as the one creator.

In *The Big-Bang Never Happened*, Eric J. Lerner writes: " . . . crucial observations have flatly contradicted the assumptions and predictions of the Big-bang. Because the Big-bang supposedly occurred only twenty billion years ago, nothing in the cosmos can be older than this. Yet in 1986 astronomers discovered that galaxies compose huge agglomerations a billion light years across; such mammoth clusterings of matter must have taken a *hundred* billion years to form." He also observes: "The cosmos evolves from chaos to order, developing more and more complex entities, in an ever accelerating movement *away* from a final, eventless equilibrium. Conventional physics views everything as a necessary regression, as devolution toward equilibrium. Yet if we look at the long term tendency of evolution, reality is just the opposite — the universe winds up, not down."

The universe is not decaying and moving towards a "heat death," but towards greater energy and increasingly complex structures. In view of the anthrophic principle — a universe created by God for man — it would seem that a slow "heat death" of the universe would also include the death of God and man. I seriously doubt that this is what God has in mind.

A concept more in keeping with the new image emerging is the one proposed by Fred Hoyle. His suggests a "steady-state" universe in which energy is constantly being created while the density of mass in the universe remains unchanged. This would relate logically to the idea of a universe that has always been and always will be, with no beginning and no end, eternally evolving through the continuous creation of atoms appearing throughout all time and space.

This explanation seems more fitting a God who has always existed, a God who has gone to such lengths to provide for us. The gentle creation of atoms throughout space would be more attuned to the gradual evolution of life on earth. A rational universe subject to precise laws suggests a final cause that does not force, or explode, or destroy, but unfolds and sustains with great and tender love all that it creates.

The evidence is telling us that one supreme Mind inhabits the universe, and without it there would be no universe. Without the intelligent organization of an infinite number of details, we would not exist. The evolution of the galaxies and stars, life and civilization, the very lawful nature of the universe itself are the result of a divinely conceived and implemented plan.

These facts challenge a purely material view of creation. However, they do not drastically change the material view as the medium we think in. They revive our faith in God, but the veil of matter cast over the mind remains, and it continues to be manifested in sin, sickness, disease, discord, adversity, lack, because we go on believing in the reality of matter as cause and law. To be free of the human belief in matter, we must understand how this intangible realm relates to our visible world. The physics of the twentieth century reveals how this is done.

ATOMS AND THE UNIVERSE

*By the word of the Lord were the heavens made; and
all the host of them by the breath of his mouth . . . .
For he spake, and it was done; he commanded, and it
stood fast.*   Psalms

*Atomic action is Mind, not matter. It is neither the
energy of matter, the result of organization, nor the
outcome of life infused into matter: it is infinite Spirit,
Truth, Life, defiant of error or matter.
Thought will finally be understood and seen in all
form, substance, and color, but without material
accompaniments. . . . God is His own infinite Mind
and expresses all.*

MARY BAKER EDDY

*The coming scientific revolution heralded the end of
dualism in every sense. Far from destroying God,
science for the first time was proving His existence —
by demonstrating that a higher, collective consciousness was out there. There need no longer be two
truths, the truth of science and the truth of religion.
There could be one unified vision of the world.*

LYNNE MCTAGGART

Chapter IV

ATOMS AND THE UNIVERSE

THE DISCOVERY of the spiritual dimension is destined to have a profound impact on individual lives. It is said today that all is consciousness; that our thinking determines our experience. We are recognizing the subjective nature of all things. Any change in how we think affects our health and well-being.

We presently believe that matter and evil are real, because we are *unconscious* of the realm of Mind. We live in and image forth a fearful, negative life because we believe we are at the mercy of the godless forces of matter. This material viewpoint will change as we develop a transcending view of the universe and man.

We can begin to experience this transition by recognizing that matter, as we think of it, is an illusion. *Atomic form and action are not illusions. The belief that material, mindless forces govern them is the illusion.* In reality, there is no matter. The veil cast over the mind is the subjective view of the universe through which we interpret energy as a godless force comprising all atomic forms. Thus we are interpreting the universe from the wrong viewpoint. Until we see beyond this illusion, we will continue to experience a mortal life of sickness, disease, age, lack, discord, and adversity. As we exchange physics for metaphysics, and become conscious of the spiritual realm, the illusion of matter fades out. By looking *through* the visible universe into the invisible realm of Mind, and adding a spiritual dimension to all things, we can exchange the material illusion for spiritual reality.

The deeper we go into the spiritual realm, the thinner the veil of matter becomes. As the nature of this spiritual realm becomes a reality to us, mindless energy and material forms will be replaced with God as the origin of all energy and form, and we will be free of the mesmerism of material cause and effect.

The image of mindless matter is nothing more than a form of mesmerism. Because this material view is so deeply embedded in consciousness, it is comparable to a hypnotic trance, a deep sleep. The mental image of matter has become a concrete form of mesmerism that will fade out as we develop a more advanced form of intelligence — one that understands atomic form and energy to be the expression of the divine Mind.

Because matter is a form of mesmerism, we can overcome it as the facts about the spiritual realm penetrate this darkened state of mind. This mesmeric illusion may seem so logical and final as to be impervious to change, but in fact, being a form of mesmerism, it has no underlying principle to sustain it.

Fortunately, we do not have to destroy a material environment in order to replace it with a better one. Matter is a hypnotic state of mind, and we de-mesmerize consciousness through an understanding of the spiritual realm. As we awaken from this false concept, matter and its laws become obsolete.

This transition takes place subjectively. It begins as we acknowledge a spiritual cause to all things. If we accept on *faith* that there is an infinite Mind underlying creation, this will not break the mesmerism of mind in matter. *We must understand scientifically how it creates, sustains, evolves, and governs all things.*

When the physics of the twentieth century discovered the nonmaterial nature of the atom, this opened a scientific path leading from the visible to the invisible realm. The physical and metaphysical realms blend into one logical concept as we accept the fact that the thought forces of Mind, and not the blind forces of matter, create and control the atom.

Because we have in consciousness a material image of all things, we visualize an objective world made up of dense, opaque, hard, heavy objects. To the five senses, it appears that all visible things are made of matter, external to consciousness; that the universe is created and evolved through non-intelligent atomic forces.

But is this true?

Consider a single atom. It is a manifestation of space and infinitesimal amounts of energy. Is there any emotion in an atom? Is there any life in it? Can it manifest intelligence, wisdom, and creativity? *Is it conscious? Can it think? No! An atom has no intelligence.* It cannot create, direct, control, or govern itself. The atom has no ability to originate an atomic form, give it life, color, beauty, individuality. One single atom does not embody any of these qualities or abilities.

Than comes the question: If a single atom does not have such qualities and abilities, how can atoms collectively have them? Can atoms, apart from a thinking cause, bond together in an infinity of different atomic structures? We believe that atomic forms are held together by mindless forces, but these fields or forces have no intelligence, creativity, or life in themselves. We assume that these forces create and maintain the universe and life, but this has never been proven. The overall picture that scientists are now piecing together indicates that a supreme intelligence controls the behavior of atoms in order to produce an infinite variety of beautiful and harmonious structures.

As the presence of a thinking cause becomes increasingly apparent, all causality must shift from a physical to a metaphysical basis. But how can a spiritual cause create and maintain the visible universe we live in?

The answer to this question begins with Einstein's discovery that mass and energy are one and the same essence. His equation $E=mc^2$ revealed for the first time that mass is crystallized or frozen energy. There is no solid substance in the universe.

Until Einstein discovered that energy and mass are the same, it was assumed that they are two different things: mass was inert, visible, and could be weighed, and energy was active, invisible, and weightless. But Einstein showed that mass is energy; it can be converted to light and heat. Energy has mass; it is affected by the pull of gravity. Mass is created where the concentration of energy is the greatest.

Einstein also discovered that mass and energy change from one state to another. This change takes place around us daily. In the striking of a match, in the burning of the sun, some amount of mass is converted into energy. When a cup of cold water is heated, it acquires mass, for it is heavier when it is hot. Mass can change to energy and energy to mass, because what appears to be solid mass is nothing more than congealed energy. The atom is empty space and energy. The few particles making up its mass are not matter as we think of it, but undulating charges of energy.

We have, then, three important facts that can be used to relate the atom to the spiritual dimension. *First, the atom has a nonmaterial structure; second, mass and energy are the same essence in different forms; and third, this essence is constantly changing from one state to another.*

There is also the growing evidence that the visible physical world and invisible realm of thought are inseparable. Thought influences physical phenomena. We are coming to find that our thinking determines our experience and affects our health. We no longer consider the body apart from the mind. It is generally accepted that fear, hatred, anger, stress, anxiety can cause sickness and disease. It is also becoming evident that prayer can heal both mind and body. The power of thought to affect the body and determine our experience has become general knowledge.

With these concepts in mind, we can consider the possibility that there is a universal Mind as the foundation to all atomic structure and action — an inexhaustible thought-source, which governs atomic energy and form with supreme intelligence. Because atomic structure has no more density than a thought or a feeling and Mind is purely mental, the visible and invisible are basically of the same medium.

The spiritual realm of Mind can relate to the atom through the mental influence it has over the atom. There are already four fields that control the atom — the gravitational field, the electromagnetic field, and the weak and strong nuclear fields. It is possible that there exists yet another field — *a spiritual field.* Like the other fields, this field cannot be detected by the senses. Yet it apparently is an all-powerful mental force that governs atomic form and action. Through intelligence, plan, order, law, and creativity, it constructs, unifies, directs, and maintains the whole of creation through thought-forces acting on atoms individually and collectively. This field originates and manifests concretely defined thoughts, ideas or images, expressed as atomic action and form.

It would be difficult to imagine a spiritual field controlling the hard, material atom as it was assumed to be over century ago. But the atom has become a nonmaterial entity, and so it is completely compatible with the nonmaterial nature of the spiritual realm. In fact, the atom's nonmaterial nature would make it inseparable from the purely mental nature of Mind. A spiritual field could sustain and control the atom because there is nothing solid in either this field or the atom. Neither is there any thought or emotion in the atom to resist the influence and control of the spiritual field. The atom has no life or inner direction of its own to oppose an infinite and all-powerful Mind. Therefore, this Mind could control the behavior of the atom without interference.

The nonmaterial nature of the spiritual field and of the atom suggests that there is no distinct separation between the thought forces of Mind and the energy and mass of the visible universe. *If mass is concentrated energy, then energy must be concentrated thought. If energy becomes mass, then it is possible that thought becomes energy, and if thought becomes energy and energy becomes mass, then atomic action and form on a universal scale would actually be the flow of thought from the spiritual field of Mind to idea to energy to mass.* The mental activity of Mind would be expressed visibly in atomic forms and their activity — just as steam, water, and ice are different manifestations of the same basic substance.

Here we have an explanation of the inseparability of the visible universe with the invisible realm of Mind. The steady-state theory suggests that energy is entering the universe from some unknown source. If a spiritual field is the source of atomic energy, this would explain where energy comes from. A spiritual field that emits energy would be the origin of the hydrogen atom that is the first step in the building of stars and galaxies, of solar systems with planets that support life. If the universe is ever expanding and at the same time creating new galaxies, then energy must be entering the universe from some unknown source. It appears evenly as a background material throughout space — it is created. At one time it does not exist, and then it does. The presence of a spiritual field filling all space would provide the steady-state theory with a source for the energy that is constantly entering the universe and becoming the hydrogen atom.

The steady-state theory suggests that there is also the presence of a *creative field* that is expressed in energy and mass. If thought becomes energy and energy becomes mass, then by adding a spiritual field to the universe, we have a source for the continuous creation of the hydrogen atom. *Mind creates energy. Energy is the effect of the mental activity of this Mind. The original hydrogen atom is the effect of this mental activity in which energy becomes crystallized or frozen as a visible entity*. Atoms could be created so effortlessly throughout space that this creative activity would take place undetected.

Mind the Only Cause or Creator

If the atom is one with the intelligence and creativity of a spiritual field, then hidden in the unseen dimension is the final controlling cause of the universe — one infinite Mind, God. If the universe is not, and never was, made of hard, round, immutable atoms, then perhaps it is not and never was made of mindless clouds of energy controlled by material forces we call fields. Now, it seems that these so-called material fields are secondary powers, subservient to the spiritual realm. *The real power of the universe rests*

(401) 767-2226   Nancy

nancy_schempp7@gmail.com

Let us be so grateful that
there is no reality to the Pain.

The Key - Deeper understanding of
God as Love.
We want to feel it

350 Goose La #141
Bldg

onally, if my mind is to be healed.

in marriage as a sacrament of the Roman
vonder if—in her heart of hearts—my ex-wife
rriage as binding.

r unbearably painful pressure and stress—that
it. I've writen of this moment elsewhere. But

e on the steps leading up to our apartment.
ound to see who was speaking to me. I looked
heard what I did (She was 18 months old—

at least a *chance* of being

ok—an odd phrasing. Yet I know that these

handwritten marginalia:
Never does separate from strength
how things are away from in sleeping
Nothing but a collection of beliefs, the belief in the medical

Yet I must also accept *my own innocence*, unco

My former wife and her parents sincerely belie
Catholic Church, eternal and unbreakable. I oft
does not to this day (30 years later) still see ou

It was six months before our separation—and
I first heard the "still, small voice" of the Holy
I will write of it again because it was so pivota

I was standing with my one-year-old daughter
The voice was so vivid, so present, that I turne
at my daughter, thinking that she surely must
perhaps she *did* hear). The voice said:

> Chad, if you leave this marriage now, you
> a happy man for your children.

It seems in retrospect an odd approach the Vo

We can let go and truly rest
on that love. We don't have to be
responsible
If I don't do what God wants me to do.
Let me see what love is really.

Kill the bullet

Law of mortal mind is so strong — Visual hearing.

"Confidence brings definition."

"One with God is a majority."

Ann Beals

in Mind. This spiritual field is the primary or governing field with the four other fields secondary and controlled by it.

With the presence of a spiritual field throughout all time and space, then the thought-forces of Mind could create, through atomic energy and form, the whole of the universe. It is known that gravity, electromagnetism, the weak and strong nuclear forces are universal, but these are now secondary or lesser fields. The universe unfolds as the result of the mental influence that the spiritual dimension exercises over its own atomic creations through these secondary fields that reside in the spiritual field. Thus, the idea of a spiritual foundation to creation can replace the image of a mindless universe of matter with a new image of a spiritual universe of Mind.

This new viewpoint restores faith in God without sacrificing the scientific progress we have made so far. The underlying thought field that creates and governs atomic structure and behavior is Godlike, spiritual. It is harmless because it is of God. The strength that binds all atoms into one infinite creation is spiritual, a supreme thought dimension, consciously giving form and action to all things. This hidden realm, complete within itself, is known as God.

If mass is congealed or crystallized energy, then all energy could be crystallized thoughts, God's thoughts manifested as the universe and man. God is cause, and creation is effect. They are one and inseparable. The cause, being harmonious and perfect, must express an effect that is harmonious and perfect. And in fact, the exquisite design and mathematical precision of God's creativity manifests harmony and perfection in those phenomena *over which the human mind has no influence.* Where God is alone in His work, He unfolds the universe in all its beauty and perfection, and does this so gently, lovingly, and intelligently that we are unaware of His hand in it. There is no struggle, violence, conflict, or force in His creativity. We live in a benign universe. Harmless energy is generated by Mind as the effect of pure intelligence and love, and creates a universe that is wholly good.

Both cause and effect are basically thought. There is in reality no dense, hard, opaque matter, but rather congealed energy producing a harmless, weightless universe and man. How much weight is there in a thought? None. Theoretically all the atoms in the universe do not weigh as much as a feather.

The proven presence of Mind resolves the dilemma of quantum mechanics. With quantum mechanics came the loss of determinism or predictable cause and effect. Physicists discovered that in the subatomic world, under identical circumstances, particles will act in unpredictable ways. Atoms in large numbers will have a predictable effect, but there is no way of predicting what a single particle will do. The discovery of this washed away the foundation of absolute cause and effect underlying the universe.

One of today's leading physicist, Freeman Dyson, stated the idea this way, "Atoms are weird stuff, behaving like active agents rather than inert substances. They make unpredictable choices between alternative possibilities according to the laws of quantum mechanics. It appears that mind, as manifested by the capacity to make choices, is to some extent inherent in every atom."

By pressing through the atomic and subatomic world and adding a divine Mind as the governing influence over all atomic form and action, we have a new foundation for the atomic world. It is possible that the unpredictable nature of atomic behavior enables God to govern all things according to His will. The controlling force is mental, not physical, and can only be understood metaphysically.

If intelligence, design, plan, direction, law and order are ever-present, then certain circumstances would cause the particles and atoms to act in a certain way, and different circumstances would produce a different effect. The cause governing this action is not physical, but spiritual, and the atoms are constantly adjusted to produce the most harmonious results possible under the circumstances. There is a final cause for all atomic action — it is one of supreme intelligence, divine wisdom, and eternal love.

The spiritual dimension is so difficult to detect because of its *omnipresence*. We live in the unchanging presence of God's intelligence and love. We cannot sense this presence because we live in it. It is like a fish in a pond. The fish lives in water, but it has never seen water. It has seen rocks and sand and other fish, but never water. Even so, all things in the universe are in Mind. We cannot go beyond it, or know of life without it, and so never being outside it, we have never actually seen it.

To give another example of God's ever-presence, we can compare it to the rotation of the earth. The earth's spinning is an ever-present motion. It never ceases or varies, and so to the unenlightened mind the earth stands still and the heavens move around it. But whether one is aware of it or not, the earth spins. We have never known a time when the earth stopped spinning and the sun stood still. By comparison, the presence of the spiritual dimension does not ebb and flow, come and go. There is no absence with which to compare its presence. It is a constant in the universe — a spiritual presence that never falters, never changes, is never withheld. It is self-perpetuating, self-sustaining, self-expressing. We do not know what it is like to live outside of its presence. It is forever here in the eternal now.

The Spiritual Process of Creation

As we look through all visible form to the Mind beneath, we arrive at one cause and creator. The cause is spiritual. The logic, creativity and supreme intelligence of a divine creator is the only possible explanation for the universe. No material cause could have laid the foundations of the heavens and the earth. They must have been created by a divine Principle, a rational Being of supreme intelligence and love. Transcending the material belief that matter and mindless forces are the origin of all things, we must conclude that the universe began spiritually. *If all things have their origin in a nonmaterial cause, this means that they must begin as a mental image or idea in this hidden realm.* If visible forms

were actually solid matter — made of billiard-ball atoms of the past
— there would be no logical way to explain how a spiritual cause
could image forth a material form. But there is no solid matter, only
empty space and clouds of energy that congeal into what appears
to be something solid. Here we begin to find answers to the questions: How did all things come into being in the first place? How did
God create a solar system with an earth that works so perfectly?
Where does life come from? How would such acts of creation take
place?

Divine creativity is a spiritual process. We could say that
God creates from the inside out. We presently believe that the
universe generates mindless matter in the form of atoms. Through
forces acting on these atoms, they become an infinite variety of
forms, some having the gift of life. Thus the entire universe seems
to begin materially and gradually evolve into increasingly complex
forms. Yet the questions arises: How do some atoms know how to
become roses and some to become robins? Who plans and guides
the creation of the endless variety of forms we see? Do the original
seeds and eggs come from a divine source? If so, how would this
Mind create them?

We could define this creative process as beginning subjectively in the one Mind with an idea which is to be imaged forth
objectively. Such divine creativity would be a process similar to our
own creative efforts. We begin with an idea which we plan to
express objectively, such as a painting. If we are going to paint a
picture, we begin by entertaining the idea, and nurturing it until we
have a good mental image of what we want to express. Then we
express the idea as a picture, working on it until we feel it is a
complete expression of what we had in mind.

In the spiritual process of creation, the one infinite Mind
begins with an idea. This is the first step in the unfoldment of Mind-
to-idea-to-energy-to-form concept. Since God is Mind, He is a thinking cause, and this Mind must be comprised of ideas destined to be
manifested as visible, tangible objects. Thus, creation would begin

with the idea first taking form as a mental image in Mind. As the idea becomes a distinct and complete concept in Mind, it begins to generate energy as the result of the creative thinking of Mind. Continuous mental activity would produce a field of energy containing the idea because the thought would become energy. As the idea develops it generates more energy.

As this energy grows stronger, it begins to image forth a vague, nonmaterial outline of the idea. This could begin as a faint or ghostlike three-dimensional image, a hologram impression barely visible as a transparent form that expresses the idea visualized by Mind. Mary Baker Eddy has written, "In sacred solitude divine Science evolved nature as thought and thought as thing."

In this creative process, the human mind is not present to influence or interfere with the unfolding idea. It is strictly between God and the idea that is to reflect Him. And so the original idea develops without obstruction or resistance as the creative process continues. As the energy imaging forth the outline grows stronger, the vague form becomes more distinct, until it begins to be solid substance. The idea grows more solid as the energy generated by Mind increases, until this very condensed field of energy becomes crystallized energy appearing as a visible, tangible manifestation of Mind.

In this way the one Mind works from the inside out, beginning with the idea and generating the energy that gradually grows stronger until it is a three dimensional form. There would be no limit to such creativity originating subjectively in the one Mind. Each idea would appear effortlessly, gradually, and gently, until it becomes a complete idea with form and color and even life.

In Genesis we read of the seed within itself. This suggests that living things have not only the gift of life, but also the ability to reproduce themselves. This reproductive process is again governed by the one Mind, for there are no material causes or laws to regulate and direct such a complex process. Nature rests in the care of God who creates and evolves it throughout all time and space.

God, Mind, the Origin of Life

It was once assumed that life would someday be created in the laboratory, but the complexity of even the smallest cell has made it clear that this cannot happen. Living things are too carefully designed to be the result of material cause and effect. Then where does life come from? As we probe the hidden realm, we will find that life comes from the living Being present in it.

If God is a living, thinking cause, then He would be the source or origin of all life. The same laws operating in the atom are the same laws operating in the farthest reaches of space. Therefore, the same Mind creating and sustaining the planet we live on must be the same Mind that is at work throughout the heavens, and would be the Mind that put life here on earth, for there is no other source for it. If God is a living God, then imparting life would be a natural act on His part. If He has gone to such great lengths to design and create a universe as a home for man, then He would certainly put man in it.

No material theory has been able to explain how life came about. There is nothing in atoms individually or collectively that gives them the power to create a living thing with a consciousness that is aware of its own being. Conscious life must originate in the hidden realm of Mind. Both animate and inanimate forms are created from the same atoms. However, because animate forms are given the gift of life, they reflect more of the one Mind than do inanimate forms.

As we press through living forms into the unseen realm underlying them, it is likely that the presence of life is related more to spiritual laws and qualities, than to physical forms and forces. *The body is the effect rather than the cause of life.* If we have a spiritual field for the atom, we would then have a spiritual field for life as well. If we look through living things and see an underlying thinking cause as their source, we find a more logical origin for life

54

than chemistry and electricity. If the spiritual dimension is one with atomic action, it must be one with all living things, making Mind the source of life.

Life is lived in the spiritual field. Atomic structures that include life are embedded in this Mind as tangible ideas or crystallized forms of energy. Although seemingly dense and opaque, they are actually empty space and clouds of energy. Viewing a living form objectively, as we do, it appears to be solid, dense, and impenetrable. But to the Mind in the spiritual realm, physical forms are transparent and present no barrier to Mind. A living body is like a hologram — a cloud-like form of harmless energy. This form, being transparent to Mind, both the individual mind and body are easily accessible to the influence of Mind. Thoughts in the Mind that is God are one with the individual mind that reflects Him, because the spiritual dimension penetrates the innermost mental recesses of a living thing. Because Mind and all atomic structure are inseparable as cause and effect, no physical body presents a solid barrier to the healing and regenerating thought-forces of this Mind.

The Irresistible Dawn of the New Age

As the illusion of matter fades, we do not find a vacuum — nothing. The spiritual realm hidden by the veil of matter comes to light, bringing with it the scientific laws underlying the healing works of Christ Jesus. This realm, which seems impersonal and even remote, becomes very near and dear as we learn that we can turn to it and find enlightenment, comfort, peace, and healing.

It is here in the healing power of this dimension that we become convinced of God's presence and find our personal relationship to Him. Because of the ethereal nature of all atomic form, we live in a mind and body totally accessible to the healing power of the one Mind. As a better understanding of God and man is revealed to us, the inmost thoughts and emotions are spiritualized, and this change in consciousness brings about healing.

The present image of a material creation, so deeply ingrained in consciousness, seems logical because it rests on what are assumed to be concrete scientific laws. But the anthropic principle indicates the first unravelings of this thought-structure. At one time the old theological view of a static universe and a supernatural creator was accepted as truth by mankind until the Scientific Age brought a tidal wave of new knowledge that swept away the darkened thought of medieval times. And now we are pressing beyond the physical into the metaphysical universe of Mind. Whether we recognize it or not, we are going to experience the same irresistible flood of new knowledge. The spiritual dimension, like the scientific dimension, relates to the whole of creation — including man himself.

It is most likely that the Theory of Everything will someday be revealed, tying together the four forces of nature into one beautiful equation, further emphasizing the harmony and perfection of God's creation. But it will not enable us to "heal the sick, raise the dead, cleanse the lepers, and cast out demons." Only an understanding of the healing power in the spiritual realm will enable us to do this.

THE SPIRITUAL REALM DEFINED

Thine, O Lord, is the greatness, and the power, and the glory, and the victory, and the majesty: for all that is in the heaven and in the earth is thine; thine is the kingdom, O Lord, and thou are exalted as head above all.

I CHRONICLES 29:11

God creates and governs the universe, including man. The universe is filled with spiritual ideas, which He evolves, and they are obedient to the Mind that makes them.

MARY BAKER EDDY

Science without religion is lame; religion without science is blind.

ALBERT EINSTEIN

Chapter V

THE SPIRITUAL REALM DEFINED

IN THEIR SEARCH for the Theory of Everything, scientists seem to visualize this equation as the ultimate explanation of all things. Because so many secrets of the universe have been revealed through equations, unifying the four fields into one beautiful equation seems logical, and probably it will happen. Stephen Hawking writes in *A Brief History of Time*: "If we do discover a complete theory, it should be understandable in broad principle by everyone, not just a few scientists. Then we shall all, philosophers, scientists, and just ordinary people, be able to take part in the discussion of why it is that we and the universe exist. If we find the answer to that, it would be the ultimate triumph of human reason — for then we would truly know the mind of God."

However, an equation seems too simple an answer for explaining the universe and life. Linking four fields into one final field could be the greatest accomplishment of science, but a Theory of Everything would not explain the harmony and perfection of creation, the evolution of life, the development of civilization, and the miracles of the Bible. The one Mind that inhabits all time and space must be far more than a mathematician. As Sir Arthur Eddington once remarked, "We should suspect an intention to reduce God to a system of differential equations." The Mind that is the foundation of the universe must surely embody the moral and spiritual qualities that the Scriptures attribute to God.

From what we are now learning about this realm, it is one of such supreme intelligence, wisdom, beauty, harmony and perfection that our present mentality is little more than a flickering candle compared to the brilliant light pouring from the one Mind, and this Mind is as close to us as our own thoughts, for it is the "kingdom of God" within us that Christ Jesus referred to. As this light penetrates the darkness within, it spiritualizes consciousness.

We need this spiritual light because the physical sciences alone cannot prevent disease or age in the body, or instill wisdom and love in the heart and soul of humanity. Nor does the recognition of the spiritual realm automatically remove the veil of matter that is the cause of all our cares and woes. The hope of a better life must now be transferred from physics to metaphysics, and here again we encounter the unexpected.

The spiritual dimension is not like the modern mind, any more than the scientific dimension resembled the medieval mind. To know the Mind of God, we can begin with those qualities within our own consciousness that relate in some degree to the one Mind. Then, through the study of Christian Science, we can develop an understanding of God and our relationship to Him, for Mrs. Eddy writes of "a divine influence ever present in human consciousness." This "divine influence" speaks to us subjectively, and is found in the inmost thoughts of the individual. We must think and pray our way into this nonmaterial realm, for there is no other door through which to enter.

As we come to understand this Mind, we begin to embody in consciousness an advanced intelligence or a spiritually scientific enlightenment that will eventually become one universal body of knowledge, as diversified as mathematics in its application to human needs, yet all resting on one absolute Principle.

This new knowledge will evolve as science and religion meet and merge into an elementary form of divine metaphysics. We will know when we have a correct understanding of this realm as it will bring about healings comparable to those of early Christianity. They will come about through spiritual means alone. Thus our healings will be proof that our understanding of the spiritual dimension is scientifically correct. As our understanding of this realm unfolds, the healing works will grow increasingly effective, harmonizing and perfecting all avenues of human experience.

A Scientific Approach to the Spiritual Realm

The anthropic principle was destined to be the outcome of the scientific age, although there was no way of foreseeing this. Because of my study of Christian Science, I knew that material cause and effect could not be a correct explanation for the universe and man. But the anthropic principle took me by surprise. When I first learned that this principle had appeared through eloquent equations and the presence of design and plan throughout the universe, my first reaction was one of awe that God should use the sciences to bring to light His presence, and that He should do it in such an ingenuous and irrefutable way. How better to convince the doubting Thomas than by presenting scientific proof of His presence and power! How better to lead the world into a renewed faith in Him, and open the way for science and religion to become one. How exciting that this door should open at a time when important scientific discoveries are becoming a thing of the past.

With the proof of this hidden realm coming through the physical sciences, and with our minds so steeped in materialism, it would be natural to interpret this realm as an impersonal structure of scientific laws — hard, rigid, unyielding, fixed, cold, and precise. A Mind that calculates the force of gravity to one part in 10^{-40} seems too exact to be involved in the dynamic affairs of humanity. We may be inclined to view this dimension as a mirror image of the material universe — a Mind that is governed by its own scientific laws and unable to relate to the individual needs of mankind. But these scientific laws are designed to create and maintain a place for man to live. Our earth is not merely a place that insures the survival of life. It is a home filled with such provision for our well-being that it calls for a divine creator. We can assume therefore that scientific laws are not the *whole* of God.

This Mind is far more than a mathematical blueprint of the universe. Mathematical precision is only part of this unseen realm.

61

A watchmaker is more intelligent than the watch he creates. Even so, the Mind of the great Watchmaker must be infinitely beyond anything we can envision.

We can approach this realm through an avenue we already understand — that of laws. The universe and man are governed by laws that are absolute. To further define this realm, the laws of God can be divided into three categories: scientific, moral, and spiritual.

The Scientific Laws of Mind

The spiritual dimension embodies scientific laws that are the same throughout all time and space. All things are created and controlled by laws so absolute that the universe can be defined in mathematical terms. A creation so consistent and rational must have an underlying cause that is also consistent and rational. The realm of Mind could not be supernatural, fickle, incomprehensible, unpredictable, vacillating, irrational, and yet produce a creation that is orderly, planned, unified, and scientific. An erratic cause cannot produce a stable effect. If Mind creates the same universe today as it did "in the beginning" and governs it with the same laws, then God, Himself, must be immutable and immortal. The plan, direction, unity, and order of the universe must come from a scientific Mind. This Mind never fluctuates, never changes. It is reliable, consistent, responsible, trustworthy, and exercises a controlling influence that is constant, never deviating from the scientific principles it has established.

Scientific laws provide a stable environment for all living things, one that reflects the Mind creating it. There is nothing fickle, erratic, chaotic, disorderly or uncertain in the universe as we have come to know it. It is stable, predictable and reliable. Scientific laws are absolute, and we are blessed by them to the degree that we understand and obey them. They express the scientific nature of the one Mind that inhabits eternity.

The Moral Laws of Mind

By understanding and obeying scientific laws we have opened the way for humanity to rise above ignorance, toil, poverty, famine, and other forms of adversity. But we have yet to realize that there are moral laws in the universe as absolute as scientific laws. To resolve problems beyond the reach of science and technology, we must abide by these moral laws as carefully as we do scientific laws.

All moral laws originate in the one Mind. God creates a stable scientific universe because He is not a mixture of good and evil, material illusions and spiritual reality, of chaos and order, of scientific and supernatural causes. Neither is He a mixture of moral and immoral traits, of positive and negative emotions. The nature of the spiritual dimension can be understood only through laws and qualities that are morally perfect. These moral laws, like scientific laws, do not fluctuate to suit the prevailing mode of world thought. The Ten Commandments are as inviolate today as when Moses recorded them. The moral laws condemning adultery, stealing, lying, killing are as absolute as the scientific laws governing the speed of light and the force of gravity. If we disobey God's moral laws, we are closed out of the spiritual realm. We live in the mental darkness of what Mrs. Eddy once referred to as the "medieval period of metaphysics." We cannot find enlightenment and healing for those problems that are beyond science and technology until we obey the moral laws of God.

When Christ Jesus taught equality, unselfed love, humility, forgiveness, compassion, honesty, integrity, justice, and obedience to the law of Love, his authority came from the fact that these qualities define the moral nature of Mind.

The human mind, with its material views and mortal traits, is unstable, discordant, sick and sinful. But the spiritual dimension does not have any erratic, discordant, immoral elements. It has no inner conflict. It is morally perfect, and the moral strength and soundness of Mind produces a universe governed by scientific laws. *Moral laws are not relative. They are as absolute as scientific laws.* The first requirement in understanding the realm of Mind is that we obey the moral laws of God. They are not beyond knowing. The Bible defines them in plain language, and in so doing becomes an indispensable key to the hidden realm of Mind.

At this point an image of the spiritual dimension begins to take form. Absolute scientific laws and incorruptible moral laws make the divine Mind quite different from our own mentality. However, scientific and moral laws do not explain the whole of Mind. There are spiritual laws as absolute as scientific and moral laws, and these form the foundation upon which all moral and scientific laws rest. And they define God.

Three States of the Human Mind

As we begin to define the spiritual laws and qualities of God, we are moving from the material and mental viewpoints into a spiritual state of consciousness.

The *material viewpoint* is one entirely convinced of the reality of matter. It recognizes only material or godless laws and forces, and bases its knowledge on the discoveries of the physical sciences for these seem to prove this view to be correct.

The *mental viewpoint* recognizes the human mind as an influence or cause that affects physical phenomena for better or for worse, but it is unaware of the spiritual realm and its laws. It cannot draw to any extent on the healing power of this realm because it does not understand it. It is basically the exercise of mind over matter.

The *spiritual viewpoint* is one that understands the laws, qualities and content of the hidden realm of Mind. As we come to discern the true nature of God, we renovate the inmost thoughts and feelings, and this spiritualizes consciousness. Material and mental impressions fade out because this advanced intelligence or new knowledge unfolds, for both the material and spiritual view cannot occupy the same mind at the same time.

The Spiritual Laws and Qualities of Mind

How do we define God? This is the purpose of Christian Science — to tell us what God is. To do this, Mrs. Eddy took from the Scriptures six terms used to define God — Mind, Spirit, Soul, Life, Truth, and Love. To these she added one more term, Principle, making a total of seven synonyms for God. In *Science and Health* she defines God as "The great I AM; the all-knowing, all-seeing, all-acting, all-wise, all-loving, and eternal; Principle; Mind; Soul; Spirit; Life; Truth; Love; all substance; intelligence." Also in answer to the question, "What is God?" she writes, "God is incorporeal, divine, supreme, infinite Mind, Spirit, Soul, Principle, Life, Truth, Love."

These seven synonyms are the key to the spiritual dimension, for they define the laws, qualities, structure and content of the Mind that occupies this hidden realm. Through these synonyms the nature of Mind takes on definite form and meaning, and an accurate knowledge of God gradually unfolds.

In analyzing the spiritual dimension through these synonyms, we can see that the final cause of all things is not matter or electricity; it is not mind over matter. It is the thought-forces of a supreme Being, who relates to the universe as the one and only creating and governing power, and who relates to man as a wise and loving Father-Mother God. Through the synonyms we begin to "know the mind of God." Each synonym accurately defines certain qualities and laws of God. *Combined they enable us to become* **conscious** *of the spiritual dimension we now live in.*

So important are these synonyms that we need to consider each one as it is used to define God. The following is a very brief explanation of these seven synonyms to acquaint you with the special qualities that each represents.

Mind: Mind is the thinking cause that creates the atom, forms the stars and flowers, and continuously carries forward a dynamic universe. This omnipresent, omniscient, omnipotent Mind manifests infallible intelligence in all that it creates and governs. The universe has never been the product of chance and material laws. It has always been consciously created by the one Mind. So perfect is its work that its creation has been mistaken for machinery. This Mind is capable of creating and maintaining a harmonious universe because it acts independently of the human mind. *It works from within and through atomic form and action to produce a dynamic creation.*

It is difficult to discern the presence of this Mind because it is pure thought, a divine intelligence that cannot be detected by the five senses. As an illustration of the presence of this universal thinking cause, let us imagine a sheet of paper covered with profound equations. Someone with no knowledge of physics would see only paper and ink. To a physicist the paper and ink would take on great meaning. Even so, when we are unconscious of God's presence, we look on the world around us and see only a three dimensional environment void of any mental cause. But as we learn more of the Mind underlying the universe, we begin to see this thinking cause, this supreme intelligence, at one with all things, including our own existence. This Mind is infinite. There is nothing beyond it. We live in an atmosphere of divine intelligence and infallible wisdom. Mind is as close to us as our thoughts. We are inseparable from it.

This Mind is the source of all right ideas — spiritual ideas, creative ideas, intelligent ideas, practical ideas — all backed by the power and presence of the one Mind. These ideas simply appear in consciousness. At one time they are not known, and then they are. They are the ideas of Mind unfolding as our own thoughts. In *Science and Health* Mrs. Eddy defines angels as "God's thoughts passing to man." This inner communication with God is indestructible because it is maintained by God, not man. Through it, God relates to our needs, answers our prayers, heals and protects us, and makes us aware of His presence. In *Science and Health*, Mrs. Eddy writes of this synonym, "Infinite Mind is the creator, and creation is the infinite image or idea emanating from this Mind. If Mind is within and without all things, then all is Mind; and this definition is scientific."

The development of civilization is the result of Mind imparting spiritual and scientific ideas to individual consciousness. The laws of physics, the power of gravity, the principles of aerodynamics have always been known to Mind, and in the Scientific Age they became known to man. Through the continuous unfoldment of new ideas, the Scientific Age will slowly evolve into the Spiritual Age, and we will discern the origin and nature of all things real to be created, governed and maintained by the one Mind, God.

Love: Why is the spiritual dimension so hidden and so difficult to understand? One reason is that God is pure Love. The spiritual realm is nonviolent. There are no negative emotions, no hostile motives, no hateful, aggressive, stressful forces in Mind. God, Mind, creates and sustains all things through the harmless power of Love. The silent creation of the atom, the gradual building of all atomic forms throughout the universe, the slow, gentle process of evolution are evidence of an unlabored activity underlying the visible universe. This creative work comes about without force, conflict, violence, or stress. It is done with supreme intelligence and pure love.

Divine Love is not far off, but intimately involved with all things. Should the disposition of divine Love embody both good and evil qualities, it would have a negative and harmful influence on what it creates, resulting in a discordant, unstable universe. An all-powerful Mind of such duality would inflict on living things suffering conditions from which they could never hope to escape. But the unseen realm is scientific, moral, and spiritual, and its laws are enforced by the gentle power of Love.

If the Love that fills the universe is as close to us as our thoughts, then it cannot be cold and impersonal. Love must love, and it must relate to that which it loves. And so God is a personal God — a living Being who knows our every need and supplies it. To the extent that we understand and obey His laws, and *listen from within* for His voice, He can unfold infinite good into our lives in the same practical way He cared for the prophets and apostles of ancient times.

Divine Love is a law to the spiritual realm. It never changes, never falters, is never withheld. This Love is different from human sentiment which can change to hate, fear and indifference. Divine Love is not a materialistic, sensual, personal sentiment. Love is the governing Principle of all that is real. "Divine Love is infinite. Therefore all that really exists is in and of God, and manifests His love," Mrs. Eddy writes in *Science and Health*.

Divine Love expresses care, patience, wisdom, gentleness, tenderness, compassion, understanding, purity, forgiveness, mercy, goodness and affection. God relates to His creation through the qualities of Love, and this Love remains forever Love. It is basic to the perfect functioning of the universe.

Mrs. Eddy describes the all-embracing realm of Love as the governing power of creation, expressing itself in beauty, harmony, and perfection. She writes of this synonym, "All things are created spiritually. Mind, not matter, is the creator. Love, the divine Principle, is the Father and Mother of the universe, including man. . . . Thus the ideas of God in universal being are complete and forever expressed, for Science reveals infinity and the fatherhood and motherhood of Love."

Truth: Christ Jesus said, "Ye shall know the truth, and the truth shall make you free." But what is truth? The desire to know truth has brought about many forms of knowledge believed to be Truth at that time, but they were eventually replaced by more advanced theories. This ongoing change and the fact that ultimate Truth has not yet been attained, raises the question: Can absolute Truth be known?

We find in Christian Science absolute Truth. There is one Mind, one Principle, one universe, and so there is one Truth. Truth comes with an understanding of the spiritual dimension. This spiritual understanding transcends present knowledge, and reveals the absolute Truth about man and the universe: *that God, good, is All-in-all; that man and the universe are the spiritual creations of God; that matter and evil are hypnotic illusions.* We know now that matter is not what it seems to be — hard, dense, heavy, and opaque. So we will learn that evil is also a false concept, a form of hypnosis that is not real, and our spiritual progress over the coming centuries will verify this fact. As world consciousness grows stronger in the truth about God and man, evil and matter will grow progressively less until they disappear entirely.

Without an understanding of the spiritual nature of reality, we have partial truths and erroneous theories. The purpose of Truth is to define reality. It is the foundation to all that exists in the spiritual realm. *Science and Health* states: "The only excuse for entertaining human opinions and rejecting the Science of being is our mortal ignorance of Spirit, — ignorance which yields only to the understanding of divine Science, the understanding by which we enter into the kingdom of Truth on earth and learn that Spirit is infinite and supreme." Truth dispels the material illusions as it reveals the whole of reality.

Truth also enforces the moral laws of honesty, justice, mercy, integrity and righteousness. It discerns in the heart of consciousness our inmost thoughts and feelings which cannot be hidden from God. The Scriptures often refer to God as just and righteous. We can understand the spiritual realm only as we are honest, just, and righteous ourselves, and harbor no desire to be otherwise. Obedience to moral laws precedes spiritual enlightenment. As we obey the moral laws of God, and think and pray our way into the realm of Truth, the mesmerism of evil and matter is broken and the illusion dies out.

Spirit: The natural sciences have passed through the visible universe without finding a final material cause. The universe is so complex that we can no longer believe it has been created out of nothing. Neither material nor mental causes can explain it. Therefore, we arrive at a non-tangible cause that is neither material nor mental, but divine, and so Spirit is a perfect term for defining this ultimate nonmaterial cause.

Spirit is more than a refined human mentality. Spirit defines the true substance of the universe. Whereas we have assumed mindless material fields and laws to be the controlling forces of creation, we need now to see atomic form and action as governed by qualities and laws which are the intelligent thought-forces of Spirit, God.

Spirit is the substance of the universe, the essence of all things real, that which underlies the visible manifestation. Substance is permanent, unchanging. The eternal qualities, laws, and energies of Spirit are the substance of all things. They form the permanent foundation of the universe. While the universe is always unfolding as the manifestation of Mind, the underlying laws and qualities remain eternally the same.

The relationship of Spirit to man and the universe can be compared to the relationship of the principle of mathematics to all mathematical problems. The principle of mathematics can be expressed in an infinite number of ways without becoming depleted. Even so, the indestructible thought-forces of God are the substance of creation. The qualities of intelligence, creativity, plan, direction, unity, law and order can be expressed forever without becoming exhausted, destroyed, changed, or obstructed because there is no matter in them to wear out. And so man and the universe must go on eternally as the effect of this spiritual cause.

In *Science and Health* Mrs. Eddy writes of Spirit, "The fading forms of matter, the mortal body and material earth, are the fleeting concepts of the human mind. They have their day before the permanent facts and their perfection in Spirit appear."

The one spiritual cause has created a nonmaterial universe. Spirit and its creations have no more solid substance than a thought or a feeling. Therefore, being nonmaterial, man's entire being is open to God's thoughts. God can reach him from within since there is no matter to obstruct this communication of thoughts from God to man.

Once we become aware of this "divine influence" within, we can turn to it for every need. The influence of Spirit, Mind, reaching the inmost thoughts, is the personal relationship that the one God has with each of us.

Thus we are one with the spiritual dimension we live in — this thought realm of divine intelligence and pure love. Because it is spiritual, it is everywhere. We can turn to it at all times for healing and protection, for enlightenment and inspiration, and it is always present to answer our prayers.

Life: If God is a thinking cause, then He is a living cause and must be the origin of life. Life does not originate in lifeless matter. It is not a product of a chemical or biological process. Material forces acting on ethereal clouds of energy could not create the infinite forms of life we find in nature, nor could they ultimately image forth man in God's likeness. With a living, spiritual cause underlying creation, it seems inevitable that life should appear as part of God's plan, and that the search for the source of life must end in an understanding that God is Life.

As a thinking cause, Mind, or Spirit, must have life-giving forces that produce living things. Mind is not passive or inert. It is active, always manifesting itself in an infinite variety of living things. Mrs. Eddy writes in *Science and Health,* "Life is divine Principle, Mind, Soul, Spirit. Life is without beginning and without end. . . . . Life is neither in nor of matter. What is termed matter is unknown to Spirit, which includes in itself all substance, and is Life eternal. Matter is a human concept. Life is divine Mind."

Life is not dependent on material cause and effect. It is

wholly spiritual, expressing the laws and qualities of the spiritual realm. If God is Life, then it would be natural for Him to create living things, and to be inseparable from them. Life is cause, and living things are effect.

God is morally responsible for all that He creates, and so He is intimately involved in the life of each of us. As we come to understand the one Mind, God's intelligence and love are manifested in our lives as health, vitality, joy, happiness, abundance, and freedom from suffering, pain, and discord. We cannot possibly plan the blessings that come to us as we emerge out of the darkness of material illusions into the realm of Life and Love. We will find ourselves under the care of a God who watches over us with warm and tender love, always aware of our every need and supplying it.

Soul: All things consist of a limited number of atomic elements arranged in an infinite variety of form and color. Since such originality cannot come from nothing, nor can it come from the mindless action and reaction of atoms, it must come from somewhere and something. It is the expression of God as Soul.

The spiritual dimension contains an inexhaustible reservoir of esthetic and practical ideas that maintain beauty and harmony in creation. This creativity remains within the framework of scientific and moral laws, while expressing design, color, form and individuality in everything everywhere.

Art, as well as Science, originates in the spiritual realm. The thought-forces of Soul express beauty, refinement, grace, elegance, splendor, harmony, and perfection that only a Godlike cause could produce. These are the special qualities of Soul expressed through intelligent creativity. Soul originates and adapts all things to their right time and place in the scheme of things.

When we watch a beautiful sunset, see birds on the wing, warm in the glow of firelight, find the first flowers in an early spring shower, we cannot help but believe that the Soul of God has made our earthly home one of breathtaking beauty and harmony.

Soul unfolds to us the ideas that reflect beauty and goodness in our lives. Not only our appreciation of beauty and perfection, but our expression of it, is God unfolding His ideas to our inmost thoughts. The more we understand God, the more freely these
creative ideas bring beauty, grace, and refinement into our lives.
They shape and form our true identity in God's image, and move
forth to transform our lives into a rich and joyous experience.

Principle: Divine Principle governs by scientific, moral,
and spiritual laws. The unity, order, plan, and direction of the universe indicates that there are not many gods and many conflicting
laws in the spiritual realm, but one Principle, God, and His perfect
laws. In *Science and Health* we read, "The creative Principle —
Life, Truth, and Love — is God. The universe reflects God. There
is but one creator and one creation."

God as Principle gives us a foundation for the scientific
universe and man — a fixed and unchanging cause that creates
and maintains a stable, lawful, unified effect. With the synonym
Principle, God becomes a universal Mind, rather than an all-powerful Person; God can be scientifically understood. The facts we learn
about the spiritual realm remain unchanging, because the realm
itself is based on absolute laws.

Gradually we will understand the spiritual dimension as we
now understand the scientific dimension, because this hidden realm
is based on an eternal Principle. At the scientific level, there are the
laws of gravity, evolution, aerodynamics, mathematics, music. At
the moral level there are the laws of honesty, integrity, morality,
humility, patience, forgiveness, compassion, and goodness. At the
spiritual level are the laws of intelligence, creativity, life, love, unity,
plan, and direction.

Although God is defined as Principle, this does not mean
that He is abstract, cold, or impersonal. Rather, it shows that God
is an unchanging Mind that we can understand and relate to. He is
reliable. We can trust Him. He is rational. He creates a universe
that we can understand. He provides moral laws for us to live by.

In her book, *Miscellany*, Mrs. Eddy writes of Principle: "What are termed in common speech the principle of harmonious vibration, the principle of conservation of numbers in geometry, the principle of the inclined plane in mechanics, etc., are but an effect of one universal cause, — an emanation of the one divine intelligent Principle that holds the earth in its orbit by evolved spiritual power, that commands the waves and the winds, that marks the sparrow's fall, and that governs all from the infinitesimal to the infinite, — namely, God. Withdraw God, divine Principle, from man and the universe, and man and the universe would no longer exist."

There are spiritual laws to govern man as there are scientific laws that govern the universe. These laws are absolute, and they operate to bless us. There is the law of health and well-being; the law of abundance; the laws of peace, righteousness, justice, mercy, purity, beauty, and harmony; the laws of love, intelligence, wisdom, and goodness; the laws of life, individuality, immortality. We presently seem to be under the mortal laws of matter and material cause and effect, with the struggle, discord, and suffering these impose on us. But as we transcend the belief in the reality of matter, and come to know the spiritual realm, then the laws of Principle govern our life. By understanding and obeying these laws, they heal and bless us. We do not have to wait for universal acceptance of these laws in order for their healing power to operate in our individual lives. We can begin here and now to come under God's laws and experience the infinite good that they bring to us.

God's law of abundance unfolds good to us individually. His law of adjustment operates to bring about the highest degree of harmony possible under the circumstances, so that our spiritual progress brings unexpected good into our life.

The laws of Principle never fail to operate to bless and prosper the individual. As we each at our own pace come to know the structure and content of the spiritual realm, these laws invariably act to bless us beyond measure.

Summary

Through these synonyms and their attributes, Christian Science gives us some concept of the spiritual dimension and man's personal relationship to it. There is in the universe a living God, Mind. This Mind is not centered in any specific locality. It is everywhere. It is not identified with any particular point in time. It is ever present in the eternal now.

The structure and content of the spiritual realm are not beyond knowing. Through the spiritual qualities in our own consciousness, we can understand the nature of God. We can learn what is in the spiritual realm and what is not. Christian Science reveals that it is not filled with a material image of creation, with cause and effect traced to matter. It is not made up of a magnified human mind, whose nature is a mixture of good and evil, truth and error, love and hate. It is not hostile, antagonistic, cold, indifferent or evil towards its own creation. It is filled with scientific logic, moral laws, and spiritual qualities. It embodies the intelligence, wisdom, and understanding of Mind; the substance of Spirit; the creativity of Soul; the law, order, unity and plan of Principle; the immortality of Life; the reality of Truth; the power and goodness of Love. This definition of God enables us to transcend the present material view, and begin to form an image of the structure and content of the spiritual dimension.

Science and Health reveals the spirituality of God and the universe with the following statements that introduce us to the true nature of God and His creation, man and the universe: "Christian Science reveals what 'eye hath not seen,' — even the cause of all that exists, — for the universe, inclusive of man, is as eternal as God, who is its divine immortal Principle."

"All reality is in God and His creation, harmonious and eternal. That which He creates is good, and He makes all that is made."

"Divine metaphysics, as revealed to spiritual understanding, shows clearly that all is Mind, and that Mind is God, omnipotence, omnipresence, omniscience, — that is, all power, all presence, all Science. Hence all is in reality the manifestation of Mind."

Because the spiritual viewpoint of creation is so radical and the material philosophy so deeply ingrained in our minds, the question arises: How do we know that this spiritual view is correct? What proof do we have that Christian Science is accurate in its analysis of God? How can we determine if this revelation is indeed fact or theory?

First, it must introduce something entirely new into world consciousness, and at the same time there must be some evidence to support its ideas. Newton's universe was based on mathematical equations. Darwin's discovery was backed by scientific research. Einstein's equation split the atom. Christ Jesus proved his teachings through his healing works.

Now, as we find ourselves facing the spiritual dimension, how can we be certain that Christian Science is the vision that correctly defines it? Proof of its authenticity is found in its healing results. Christian Science reveals the spiritual laws underlying the healing works of Christ Jesus. It restores the lost art of spiritual healing to Christianity.

THE SPIRITUAL AND MATERIAL VIEWPOINTS

How precious . . . are thy thoughts unto me, O God!
How great is the sum of them. If I should count them,
they are more in number than the sand: when I
awake, I am still with thee.

PSALMS

ANGELS. God's thoughts passing to man; spiritual
intuitions, pure and perfect; the inspiration of
goodness, purity, and immortality, counteracting all
evil, sensuality, and mortality.

MARY BAKER EDDY

At every point in the past when that final goal was
thought to be in sight, new and wholly unexplained
phenomena were soon discovered.

ERIC J. LERNER

Chapter VI

THE SPIRITUAL AND MATERIAL VIEWPOINTS

OVER THE CENTURIES there have been many different views of the same heavens and the same earth, and each was believed to be the truth. Presently we have a very material image of them, but we are beginning to develop two opposing views — the material and the spiritual. Until the spiritual realm was discovered, the material view was the only view. Now we have a choice.

The Material Viewpoint

The material view sees man and the universe created and governed by matter and its laws. Everything is the result of non-intelligent, lifeless forces. To the materialist, physical forces are assumed to be the *only* cause, so that all atomic structure and behavior exist apart from any mental influence or control. The material theory recognizes no spiritual cause, for it assumes that there is no need for one. It is a closed system of material cause and effect.

This image is presently a universal conviction. We may have great faith in God, but we still believe that matter is solid and real, and that our life is encased in it and depends upon it.

Our thoughts objectify themselves involuntarily. We relate to the culture around us because we all have the same fundamental viewpoint. We hold in consciousness images of a material life as a collective state of mind. We suffer together from this conviction because we are *unconscious* of the spiritual dimension. When the veil is heavy and thought is darkened by the belief in matter, we objectify a life that matches this inner image of discord, disease, sickness, and all that makes up mortal existence.

As long as consciousness is darkened by the conviction that matter is real, it will interpret the images it holds in consciousness to be material, and image forth a life patterned after its own ungodlike mentality. Thus, although here and now we live in a spiritual universe designed to bless man, to the mind mesmerized by the belief in matter, the subjective image is one of a material universe and a mortal man.

The age-old question, why does God allow discord, disease, and suffering, is answered as we learn of the spiritual realm. *All suffering comes from the materialized mind that is unconscious of the one Mind and man's relationship to it.*

As a rule, regardless of how religious a person may be, the universal belief in matter becomes individualized in consciousness, and the material view remains the basic view. We are then imprisoned in the illusion that matter is real and material laws control us. This view then generates harmful energy manifested in a material body and a mortal life. The stronger the material view, the more negative the energy and the more susceptible we are to sickness, disease, age, and adversity of every kind.

The Spiritual Viewpoint

We escape mortal existence as we cultivate the spiritual viewpoint, for as this viewpoint unfolds, the material view proves to be obsolete — the wrong view. By pressing deeper into the spiritual realm, we find that the divine Mind, and not the godless forces of matter, creates and governs all things. Eventually the spiritual view will be recognized as the true view, transcending the material view and replacing it.

In reality, atomic form and action are the effects of the intelligence and love of God. Thus the spiritual universe and man rest in a divine cause. It is a closed system of spiritual cause and effect. The mind that understands the laws and qualities of the one Mind and thinks and lives in them, embraces in consciousness images that are spiritual, originating in God.

The spiritualization of thought effects all the images we have within. The veil of matter thins out. We do not feel as imprisoned in material laws, when we begin to realize that underlying all things is a spiritual cause. As thought becomes increasingly educated in spiritual realities, the healing, protecting, and providing power latent in the spiritual realm is objectified in a life of affluence, health, and happiness.

Transcending the Material Viewpoint

How do we go about achieving this transcending experience? *It all takes place subjectively.* We renovate the inmost thoughts by becoming educated in divine realities. We escape pain, suffering, discord, and limitation by exchanging the material view for the spiritual view. A most important part of Mrs. Eddy's discovery is the fact that matter is an illusion, an erroneous conviction that has no real cause or origin. This mesmerism can be corrected as we become conscious of the spiritual realm.

We yield up the illusion of matter for the substance of Spirit as spiritual enlightenment changes how we think. Mankind's progress has always come about through a change in his viewpoint. Following the Dark Ages, scientific discoveries restructured man's image of the universe. Then the mechanistic universe gave way to one of chance and probability. Now this image is again changing through the discovery of an intelligent cause underlying creation. Nothing in the universe has changed over these centuries. The universe has always been governed by scientific laws. It has always been one of pure energy. There has never been anything solid about man's celestial home. Moreover, the unseen Creator has always been one with His creation, and the universe and man have always existed as the effect of a spiritual cause. To enter this heavenly realm, we need once again to change how we think.

The discovery of the spiritual dimension is much more than another scientific breakthrough. It affects the very heart of consciousness, and brings about a major transformation of our entire philosophical, religious, and scientific structure of ideas. But until we develop some understanding of the spiritual realm, the material view will remain basically the same, and the life it objectifies will continue to be one of discord and limitation.

We escape mortal life by spiritualizing our basic viewpoint. The material and spiritual views are opposite views and produce opposite images in consciousness, and so we cannot have two opposite views in the same mind at the same time. One or the other has to be the view we believe in as reality.

The subjective work of understanding God and His creation translates the mental images in consciousness from material illusions to spiritual ideas. We seem to live in a material universe and a physical body, but in the last analysis we live in mental impressions.

As an example, when we see a clock on the table, we *mentally* see it as a hard, three-dimensional object. But the clock does not actually leave the table and become a hard, three-dimensional object in our mind. It remains on the table. All we have in consciousness is *a mental image of the clock*. We think of it as a material, mechanical, useful object; yet all that we ever know about it is our mental impression of it.

This simple example applies to everything in our experience. Our entire life is comprised of mental impressions in consciousness. The clock exists on its own, whether or not we are aware of it, but it only exists to us as a mental image. How we interpret the image depends on the spiritual or material viewpoint that we hold in consciousness.

When consciousness is materialized, it visualizes objects as hard, heavy, opaque — objects that decay and die. It objectifies a mortal life dependent on material things. As the mind is spiritualized with divine intelligence and love, the images it recognizes and objectifies are seen as ideas of Mind. They are lighter, less opaque, almost transparent at times. It objectifies a life dependent upon the one Mind and its ideas.

Two Forms of Energy

These two opposite views offer an explanation of how prayer heals, protects, and prospers those who have some understanding of the spiritual realm. Christ Jesus' healing works were seen as the effect of supernatural causes, but the inseparability of mind-thought-energy-form provides a scientific basis for the "miracles" that have taken place over the centuries. The material and spiritual views have an opposite effect on our health and well being because they produce different forms of energy. We assume that energy is simply energy. But in fact, there are *two forms of energy. The material view generates harmful, destructive, negative energy, while the spiritual view generates harmless, healing, positive energy.*

The material state of mind embodies negative emotions of fear, hate, and selfishness, which in turn generate negative energy. It is the ungodlike emotions and beliefs of material-mindedness that produce harmful and lethal energy. A material view claims that we are dependent on matter, governed by its laws, limited by circumstances, and this results in hate, fear, selfishness, lust, jealousy, anger, rage, pride, self-righteousness — all the negative emotions of the darkened mind. These emit a harmful, destructive, even poisonous energy, that causes sickness, disease, pain, suffering, and all malfunctioning of the body. It brings on mental and emotional illness, crippling conditions, and old age. Negative energy is not limited to mental and physical conditions, but affects the events of our life as well. It objectifies a hard, opaque, hostile environment governed by chance, fate, and circumstances, with evil and matter the predominant forces of the entire illusion of life in matter.

The more materialistic, or godless, the mind, the more discordant, sick, and limited all that it objectifies. Because this mental darkness is so entrenched in consciousness, it embodies images of clocks and all things as heavy, hard, opaque forms.

If this material view were the right one and the only one, mankind could never hope to escape the discord and suffering of the mortal dream. But the discovery of a spiritual realm becomes the open door that frees us of the mortal dream, for we think and pray our way out of the illusion of matter into the spiritual realm.

John of Patmos sums up the nature of this hidden realm in the words; "God is love." Because God is Love, the energy He generates is a harmless, benign power that creates and animates the universe and man. This harmless energy is inseparable from its source. It never becomes harmful, lethal, or disease-producing. This energy is gentle, tender, warm, and inexhaustible in its loving care. It operates unspent. It has its source in divine Mind, and so it is intelligently directed and used. The intelligence and love of God is the thought-power of energy forming the universe and man.

As we understand this realm, we reflect affection, forgiveness, tenderness, gentleness, humility, and purity, and this in turn generates the harmless energy that heals and protects us from all adversity. This atmosphere of spiritual love then objectifies itself in lasting health and happiness.

Spiritual Healing Explained

We come now to a scientific explanation of spiritual healing. We have two different sources for energy – the material or negative, and the spiritual or positive. The nature of our individual world depends on the fundamental viewpoint we embrace in the heart of consciousness. Because there are two opposite views, they generate *two different types of energy*, depending on the viewpoint of the mind generating them. The mind-thought-energy-form is one as cause and effect. Energy cannot be separated from the mind producing it, and the form cannot be separated from the energy producing it. This relates to both views — the spiritual and the material. Therefore, the determining factor in our lives is the material or spiritual view we hold as absolute conviction in the heart of consciousness.

The material viewpoint, mesmerized with hatred, fear, self-will, material beliefs, generates electrical energy that is harmful, destructive, and death-producing. It images forth sick, diseased, decaying forms in a discordant mortal life. Until we spiritualize consciousness, we think in a material view that generates negative energy, and brings about discordant and painful experiences.

With the discovery of the spiritual dimension, the cause of incurable disease, mental illness, physical deformity, lack, discord, drug addiction, even the most entrenched mortal illusions, can be overcome through an understanding of the hidden realm of Mind and its healing power. The transcending vision destroys the effects of negative emotions and energy as it generates positive emotions and energy and harmonious images in the consciousness that reflects the divine Mind.

As thought changes from the material to the spiritual viewpoint, the energy it generates also changes, and so the harmless, constructive energy of Mind counteracts and replaces the harmful, destructive energy of matter. This energy then restores or heals the body that is inseparable from it. It changes abnormal conditions of disease and illness into health, and pain and suffering into vitality and well-being. This new state of mind then objectifies itself in a better life. *We do not spiritualize material things; we dematerialize the spiritual idea.* Thus we see how important it is to understand and think in the spiritual ideas that unfold from God, rather than the material illusions of the human mind.

Spiritualizing Consciousness

This then raises the question: How do we spiritualize thought? This comes through study and prayer. We can relate to the one Mind because there are already elements within our own mind that reflect God. We think in intelligence, order, plan, law, wisdom, justice, life, truth, and love. We could say we are a mind within Mind, an idea within a thinking Cause. Moreover, our minds can change. Thought is never so hardened or opaque that it remains impervious to new ideas.

To overcome a life imprisoned in matter and its laws, we begin in our own consciousness and challenge the illusion of matter metaphysically. At this time matter seems real and powerful. Although we may acknowledge the presence of a spiritual realm, actually renovating the inner self and seeing through the veil of matter requires more than a desire to do so. Through study and prayer in Christian Science, a more advanced form of intelligence gradually unfolds and overcomes our conviction in the reality of matter.

As we learn more about the spiritual realm, we see that God can penetrate the material illusion in consciousness as light shines in the darkness, because there is no barrier to God's thoughts when we are receptive to them. God's thoughts are more powerful than the illusion of matter. When they meet, the spiritual idea overcomes mortal mesmerism.

It may seem that the material viewpoint has grown so solid and entrenched that the inner voice has been silenced, and we face this new dimension with very little spirituality within; but no one's inner self is entirely without the "still, small voice." The desire to learn of God is enough to revive our sensitivity to the presence of this divine influence, however faint.

There are degrees of spiritual and material elements in human consciousness. Some minds appear to be so dark and negative as to seem void of any spiritual element. Still, we are all equal in God's sight, and the repentant heart is known to Him. The inner self, yearning to understand God, will find new ideas unfolding daily in the light of Christian Science.

Our oneness with God is comparable to the sketch of a rose that is one with the paper it is printed on. The rose and the paper are one and inseparable. So man and the universe are visible "sketches" in the one infinite Mind. Nothing can destroy the Mind we rest in, and we are one with it as the rose is one with the paper.

Only the mental darkness of materialism prevents us from seeing and feeling this oneness.

To free the mind of the material view, we can begin by realizing that the spiritual view alone represents reality, and therefore the material view is obsolete. God is All. Matter is hypnotic illusion. Every atom in the universe is created and controlled by God, and no amount of negative thought can interfere with God's control of the universe, or prevent the world from turning, the seasons from changing, and the sun from shining. Because in reality there is no matter to resist God's ideas, His thoughts effortlessly objectify themselves as the universe and man. Where human thoughts are excluded, nature and the universe operate harmoniously. The heavens and the earth are God's thoughts imaged forth as visible or concrete ideas. Once we see the universe in its spiritual reality, we find we live in a heavenly place without a single harmful law or element in it.

There is no barrier between God's thoughts and our own inner self. Both are mental. There is no separation between our thoughts and the energy and form that our thoughts objectify. Our thoughts influence the atomic structure and function of our body. And so a permanent cure for all our problems lies in spiritualizing the basic viewpoint within. By doing so, we have at last a way out of the mortal, material dream. Thought generates energy, and this energy becomes form. Thought and energy and form are inseparable. Energy cannot exist without the thought that generates it. Harmless thought emits harmless energy. Aggressive, fearful thought generates harmful, destructive energy.

Because the present material view seems so real, the acceptance of even some elementary truth found in Christian Science may be enough to bring about very impressive healings, because the person's thoughts and emotions have been spiritualized enough to change the physical condition. Although the material view still remains basically unchanged, enough spiritual enlightenment has taken place to relieve severe problems. However, impressive healings and great faith in Christian Science are not enough to rid consciousness of the entire material viewpoint. We must work to understand the whole of Christian Science if we are to be free of all material illusions and the suffering they cause.

Spiritual Realities Replace Material Illusions

The idea of spiritualizing consciousness sometimes brings on the fear that if we do not have a physical body and a material world, we will cease to exist, if matter were not real and present, there would be nothing to live in. But as we progress spiritually, we drain out of consciousness a false image, an illusion. As we rise above the illusion of matter, we do not create a vacuum within, or bring on the collapse of our world. If all of the negative energy were drained out of the universe this minute, the universe and man would go right on because the true cause — the one God — would continue to create and maintain creation in all of its harmony and perfection. The universe and man would not be without energy and form. They would be found in their original harmony and perfection without a single harmful element. We would then see the perfect, all-harmonious universe, which has always been here, even during the seeming presence of a material one.

While the mortal, material viewpoint is changing and changeable, temporary and imperfect, the spiritual view is infinite and eternal, forever unchanging. It cannot lapse into anything less than its own perfection. There is nothing beyond the spiritual realm. There is nothing back of the one infinite Mind.

Matter and its seeming laws are an illusion. How much weight or density is there in a thought, an idea, an emotion? None. If we took all the spiritual forms in the universe and placed them in a scale, how much would they weigh? Nothing. The universe we live in is like a hologram of visible spiritual ideas. It exists first in Mind, and then is pictured forth as a dynamic, living, evolving creation, reflecting the beauty, harmony and perfection of the one all-harmonious God. The more our consciousness is spiritualized, the more all things take on their true outline, form, and color as ideas of Mind, objectified through the pure thought of the Godlike man.

Therefore, a permanent cure for all of mankind's problems lies in spiritualizing the basic viewpoint we hold within. By doing so, we have at last a way out of the material plane of existence. As we study Christian Science and pray for enlightenment, God's thoughts reach us where we are, and transform consciousness.

This hidden realm may seem dark and opaque, but as we seek to understand it through this Science, it will reveal its secrets just as the scientific realm revealed its secrets to those with a faith strong enough to believe it would.

TRANSFORMING CONSCIOUSNESS

*And I heard a great voice out of heaven saying,
Behold, the tabernacle of God is with men, and he
will dwell with them, and they shall be his people,
and God himself shall be with them, and be their
God. And God shall wipe away all tears from their
eyes; and there shall be no more death, neither
sorrow, nor crying, neither shall there be any more
pain: for the former things are passed away.*
REVELATION 21:3

*St. John spiritually discerned and revealed the sum
total of transcendentalism. He saw the real earth and
heaven. They were spiritual, not material; and they
were without pain, sin, or death. Death was not the
door to this heaven. The gates thereof he declared
were inlaid with pearl, — likening them to the price-
less understanding of man's real existence, to be
recognized here and now.*
MARY BAKER EDDY

Chapter VIII

TRANSFORMING CONSCIOUSNESS

THE CONCEPT of Mind as the only cause may be new to the world, but this divine intelligence has been the foundation of the universe throughout eternity. Spiritually inspired individuals over the ages have intuitively used its healing power. Now this power is destined to be universally available to heal the sin and suffering of all mankind.

Basic to this salvation is the fact that thought becomes energy and energy becomes form. The three are inseparable, making form or body actually a "thought-form" that is affected for better or for worse by the mind underlying it.

To spiritualize the thoughts that affect atomic form and action, the focal point of the mind must shift from the physical to the metaphysical, from the objective to the subjective, and the inner self must be educated in divine realities. Then divine intelligence replaces the illusion of matter and evil with God as the only cause and creator. This spiritual enlightenment transforms consciousness and results in healing and regeneration.

In our inner self we presently hold both mortal and immortal thoughts and feelings, human traits and Godlike qualities, which determine the harmony or discord we objectify. Because we know so little about the spiritual realm, our minds are predominantly mortal, deeply mesmerized to believe in the power and reality of evil and matter.

This dark, negative view is so entrenched in consciousness that it generates harmful energy, which affects the body with sickness, disease, deformity, and age, and objectifies itself in a discordant, limited life. The way to be free of a mortal life is to change our basic viewpoint. However, we cannot stop thinking in a material, mortal view unless we have a *transcending vision* to replace it, and Christian Science supplies this much needed vision. Although this realm is hidden from the senses, it is not as difficult to understand as it may appear to be. Learning about it is an adventure so filled with inspiration, hope, and healing that those already engaged in the study of this Science are daily blessed by it.

Study and Prayer Essential

The work of spiritualizing consciousness begins with the study of Christian Science. God's thoughts appear as our thoughts as we study and pray, listening from within for the unfoldment of spiritual ideas that will transform our viewpoint. To do this, we need to hear the "still, small voice" maintained by God as "a divine influence ever present in human consciousness." As we open our minds to this inner voice, study Christian Science, and pray scientifically, we gradually exchange the material view for the spiritual. *Both study and prayer are essential in transforming consciousness because the most deeply entrenched mesmerism does not yield entirely through study alone.*

Prayer is the key to this hidden realm. Human reason, intellect, and logic are not enough to pry open its secrets. We are searching for a form of intelligence we have never known before, and we achieve this goal through prayer. With Christian Science as the foundation of our prayer, we can press against the edges of the mind with absolute faith that the spiritual realm will be revealed to us.

Study and prayer are based on the fact that God is All-in-all; that the universe and man are spiritual ideas in and of this one Mind; that evil and matter are mortal illusions. Evil and matter are unknown to God. Mrs. Eddy explains this fact in her profound work, *Unity of Good.* There she tells us: "As God is Mind, if this Mind is familiar with evil, all cannot be good therein. Our infinite model would be taken away. What is in eternal Mind must be reflected in man, Mind's image. How then could man escape, or hope to escape, from knowledge which is everlasting in his creator?" She also writes: "All that *is*, God created. If sin has any pretense of existence, God is responsible therefor; but there is no reality in sin, for God can no more behold it, or acknowledge it, than the sun can coexist with darkness." The more we understand God and man in His likeness, the less we believe in matter and evil, and the less we suffer from our own erroneous thinking.

The illusion of matter comes from the belief in a cause other than God. In Christian Science the illusion of a negative cause, or evil, is termed *animal magnetism*. It is the antichrist made up of the material beliefs and mortal emotions that create negative energy. As the illusion of matter dissolves, it takes with it all the negative beliefs and emotions of animal magnetism, proving that evil has neither power nor reality.

The purpose of our prayerful work is to realize the allness of God and the unreality of animal magnetism and matter. God is the only power and reality, and He alone governs man and the universe. He expresses pure and perfect energy, and creates all forms with the spiritual essence of divine thought. The hidden realm is not a mixture of good and evil, Truth and error, Spirit and matter. It is perfect Mind, pure Love, immortal Truth, and indestructible Life. We cannot detect the presence of this Mind through conflicting elements because there is no conflict in it. It is pure Love.

Obedience to Moral Laws

We begin our insight into the spiritual realm by understanding it to be the source of all *moral laws*. Obedience to moral laws radiates harmless energy, while defiance of them emits destructive energy. All moral laws originate in God and define His nature. They are not relative. They are absolute. To defy these laws, to have other gods, to be materialistic, immoral, selfish, dishonest, hateful, covetous, envious, deceitful, lustful, proud, or afraid, is to have

95

thoughts and feelings that emit harmful, disease-producing energy, which are then manifested in ill health and a discordant life. They harden the heart and darken the mind.

A mind blinded by lust, consumed by hate and self-will, or paralyzed by fear, does not have a mental atmosphere that relates to the purity and spirituality of God's thoughts. A mind obedient to Christian standards expresses the moral laws of honesty, affection, humility, kindness, compassion, justice, mercy, gentleness, forgiveness, generosity, chastity. These are qualities of Love that soften the inner self so it can be receptive to the ideas that spiritualize it. When we obey moral laws, we have taken the first step towards understanding the spiritual dimension, because obedience to moral laws precedes the more advanced understanding of this realm.

Fortunately, the majority of the Christian world obeys these moral laws to a large degree. These laws are at the very heart of Western civilization. For that reason the dawning of the Spiritual Age will come first to this Christianized thought. The healing, transforming power of this realm will grow stronger until the collective presence of this spiritualized thought gradually leavens the whole of world consciousness and brings about universal salvation.

As we obey the moral laws in the Ten Commandments and the Sermon on the Mount, the spiritual realm, "hidden in sacred secrecy," begins to unfold. Through the study of Christian Science, we learn who God is, and what He does for us. Reading and pondering the Scriptures, *Science and Health*, and other important writings on Christian Science, unfold new ideas about God and His creation, and we begin to see through the veil of matter into this invisible realm.

Simply introducing spiritual ideas into consciousness begins to de-mesmerize it. They pierce the darkness of materialism with spiritual enlightenment, and initiate our freedom from the material laws that seem to imprison us.

Our study begins with *reading Christian Science.* The Bible and *Science and Health* are the cornerstone of this study.

All correct literature regarding this Science is based on these two books. Christian Science is such a profound discovery that one can be overwhelmed by the depth of its metaphysics and the many subjects it covers. The past century has brought us a treasure-trove of books and papers on it, each giving a special insight into it. To read and ponder deeply these spiritual works is a form of prayer that begins the spiritualization of consciousness.

Focus on Christian Science Treatment

However, general study — reading and pondering Christian Science — is not enough to completely free the mind of the mesmerism of matter and animal magnetism. For centuries this hypnotic illusion has been building in world thought. If this mesmeric state of mind could be destroyed through faith in God, it would have slowly disappeared with the spread of Christianity. But it remains so aggressive and universal that it continues to hold mankind in bondage to sickness, poverty, and every kind of adversity. Even proof that solid matter does not exist, even knowing that the spiritual realm does exist, is not enough to free us of animal magnetism.

To break the illusion of evil and matter requires both a dedicated study of Christian Science and the unique form of prayer that originated with it. *It is the simple but powerful prayer of affirmation and denial, or the treatment. In this prayer, you take the initiative and affirm as truth the ideas about God and man that have come from your study, and then you vigorously deny the power and reality of matter and evil.* The power of this prayer lies in the fact that it is true — God *is* All, and evil and matter *are* unreal.

Dear Friend, *the treatment is everything!* I urge you to learn more about it from my other writings, as it is the key to the spiritual dimension. You need to read and study Christian Science to gain the letter of this Science, but to demonstrate the healing power latent in the spiritual realm you need to pray daily with the treatment. As you withdraw from the world and make God the focal point of consciousness, your work with the treatment can open up the deeper levels of the spiritual realm and bring about awesome healing results.

Because Christian Science is so infinite a subject, I will simplify this discussion by focusing on the treatment itself. This basic approach to this Science will provide a good foundation for further study and acquaint you with the form of prayer that frees consciousness of the illusion of matter, mortal traits and beliefs, and animal magnetism.

There are five main subjects in a general treatment: *God, man, matter, mortal mind, and animal magnetism*. The treatment is based in the seven synonyms for God as they relate to these main subjects.

Success in this prayerful work begins with a thorough study of each synonym through the Scriptures and Mrs. Eddy's writings, as well as dictionaries and a Thesaurus, so that you can reason on them intelligently and correctly.

The nature of the supreme Being inhabiting reality is most clearly defined in the seven synonyms given in *Science and Health*: *Mind, Spirit, Soul, Principle, Life, Truth, Love*. One of Mrs. Eddy's greatest contributions to humanity is her concise and complete definition of God. The seven synonyms are like a prism that separates light into its rainbow of colors. These seven terms reveal God's many hues, which combined define His divine nature. They enable us to understand Him.

Through the synonyms we learn that the spiritual dimension is filled with a thinking, living, dynamic Being. It is neither stagnant, neutral, nor a mixture of good and evil. It is divine Love, all-powerful Mind, indestructible Life. Jesus referred to it as the Father who hears our prayers and answers them. As we reason that God is All, and matter and animal magnetism are illusions, we begin to discern the presence of this one Mind

I have already discussed the synonyms as the key to the spiritual realm. They are also the foundation to the treatment through which we enter this realm. If we are going to find the kingdom of God within and learn the art of healing through prayer, we must make Christian Science the focal point of thought. Hours spent alone with God, reading and pondering the Truth, and working with the treatment, transforms consciousness. Since we think and pray our way into the spiritual realm, daily dedication to study and prayer is essential. This prayerful work introduces into consciousness new ideas that become an advanced intelligence, stirring the mind, enlightening and purifying it.

Treatment Defined

The treatment is a prayer of action in which you take the initiative and affirm, or argue for, the presence and power of God through the synonyms, and acknowledge man as His image and likeness through the synonyms. Then you deny, or argue against, the reality of matter, mortal mind and animal magnetism through the synonyms. The treatment is important because the mesmeric hold of animal magnetism is impressed so deeply on consciousness, that some aspects of this mesmerism will only yield as you detect its presence and aggressively reject it as real and powerful.

The most effective means of de-mesmerizing consciousness is through this scientific prayer. *The treatment is the most powerful form of intelligence on the earth today*. It is different from faith-filled prayers of the past. A prayer more powerful than one based on faith in God is needed to break the mesmerism that matter is real. And so Mrs. Eddy originated this unique approach to praying. She makes a very distinct separation between the real and the unreal, good and evil, Spirit and matter, Truth and error, and then she explains how to free the mind of evil's mesmerism by affirming God's allness and denying the reality of matter and animal magnetism.

A treatment should include the four main steps: *Affirming God through the synonyms; identifying man with the synonyms;*

denying the power and reality of matter, mortal mind and animal magnetism; and then reaffirming the oneness of God and man in His likeness.

The treatment is not a formula, but a simple outline for beginning your prayerful work. Study gives you the letter of Christian Science, and the treatment converts the letter into spiritual understanding. You will spiritualize consciousness in the heart of treatment as thought is illumined with spiritual ideas and inspiration, counteracting the belief in matter and animal magnetism. Your treatment will be progressively effective as you grow spiritually and find ways to apply it to specific needs.

The following example illustrates how your study can be used in giving a healing treatment. The treatment will focus on the allness of God and unreality of matter because that is what we are mainly concerned with at this time.

First Footstep: Relating God to the Synonyms

We begin the treatment with the definition of God from *Science and Health*: "God is incorporeal, divine, supreme, infinite Mind, Spirit, Soul, Principle, Life, Truth, Love." Then consider how each synonym reveals a special insight into the nature of God.

For example, we can prayerfully consider the synonym *Spirit, substance*. Spirit is the cause and origin of the universe and man. So, this cause, being universally Godlike, must objectify energy and form like itself. Being the only cause in the universe, it must govern and maintain its own forms in harmony and perfection, since cause and effect are inseparable. God, Spirit, cannot create a mindless universe, and there are not *two* causes for *one* universe. Therefore, the substance of all that is real originates in God, and becomes visible and tangible as creations of the one Mind. Spirit is the nonmaterial basis for a system that is wholly spiritual. If the ideas of divine Mind emit energy, which become forms, then both thought and thing are wholly spiritual, and forms must express the harmony, beauty and perfection of the Mind that creates them.

When Spirit is recognized as the only cause, this understanding takes away the heaviness and darkness of materialism. Our thoughts and our world express less of the discord of matter and more of the harmony of Spirit. As the illusion of matter dissolves, only the substance of Spirit remains, and matter disappears as the universe and man as God made them come to light.

Spirit is a perfect word to define this unseen realm, for it is not a mental cause of a material universe; it is not a metaphysical mixture of good and evil; it is a holy realm, a heavenly atmosphere of supreme goodness. In our prayerful work we begin to *sense* or *feel* this spiritual presence throughout all time and space. It is the presence in which we "live, and move, and have our being."

Next we can consider God as *Life, being*. God alone is Life and He is Spirit. True being is immortal, harmonious, indestructible because there is no matter in life to be weary, sick, or deformed. It is filled with inexhaustible good. The formations of Life, being made of divine substance, express perfect health, inexhaustible energy, indestructible being. Life fills the "eternal now" with harmony and perfection. God, Life, watches over all living things with a Father's eternal vigilance. Divine Life maintains perfect health and ageless being in man.

As the illusion of an existence apart from God is overcome, we discover that the one Father blesses us with an abundant life, anticipating our every need. Christ Jesus said, "Your Father knoweth what things you have need of, before ye ask Him." An all-knowing, ever-present, all-powerful God as Life, supplies all that is required to maintain His creation, for He is the source of every good thing. As we cultivate the habit of trusting God, His ideas unfold within thought and are imaged forth as the perfect answer to our prayers. We begin to experience our real life in God here and now.

God is *Truth, reality.* Truth is the Science that defines the nature of this one and only Cause, God. Truth is infinite, eternal, absolute, immutable. It is reality void of the illusion of matter. Truth is forever, for it is the substance of all true knowledge, the Science that never changes.

As the veil of matter is cast aside, we see that eternal Truth is the rock upon which all Science rests — the fact that God is All-in-all, and that matter, mortal mind, and animal magnetism are unreal. All things real are inseparable from the spiritual source that gives them substance, form and color, and this is the Truth concerning creation. Truth makes the spiritual nature of the universe comprehensible to us. To understand the universe and man as spiritual, not material, is the greatest freedom we can hope to have.

One synonym we are familiar with is *Love.* God is Love, the all-powerful, ever-present Father and Mother of all. Love is the source of harmless energy and the designer of perfect form. Love's giving operates unspent in providing infinite good to man, God giving all and man having all that God gives.

Love defines the *emotional* atmosphere of reality. It is the pure love of God that draws us into the spiritual realm, because Love is irresistible. As we understand and reflect Love, this frees us of the illusion of matter. The substance of the universe is indestructible good, because the energy that forms and animates all things real comes from divine Love. Love is a cause that is warm, gentle, tender, forgiving, patient, compassionate, pure, intelligent, and wise. Love is all-powerful. Its tender care, enveloping man in a love ever pure and true, supplies his every need, and there is no opposite attraction in reality to separate man from this infinite source of all good. Love cares for all living things with untiring devotion. The universe is harmless and holy, for it is of Love, and divine Love could not create or emit harmful, destructive energy that inflicts pain and suffering on its own creation. Love brings to man a joyful life, perfect health, and every good thing.

As we discern the spiritual realm, we find God is *Mind,* *intelligence, wisdom and understanding.* All substance is the manifestation of intelligent ideas made visible. Mind is one with the forms it creates, and governs them with divine intelligence and infallible wisdom.

Divine intelligence is the substance of man's being. It includes spiritual ideas, creative ideas, intelligent ideas, and practical ideas. To the extent that the individual mind thinks in this intelligence, the life he expresses is harmonious in every way. He draws upon this unlimited source of good, which unfolds subjectively, and uses it to live his life in harmony with the one Mind.

The universe and man are individual ideas held in the one Mind in an infinite variety of forms. Because Mind is All-in-all, ideas are unfolding constantly throughout the universe. Mind governs this unfoldment, and all ideas are perfectly designed to fulfill God's plan and purpose for them. As thought becomes energy and form, the one Mind is inseparable from the thought, action and form it creates, and so it governs the effect of its own thoughts with divine wisdom and intelligence. Mind planned and designed the universe as a home for man, and remains forever its supreme governing power, the sole source of all substance and energy.

By exchanging faith for spiritual understanding, we evolve beyond the natural sciences into a more elite form of intelligence. We begin to communicate more freely with Mind and demonstrate more of its intelligence, wisdom, and spiritual understanding.

The universe is governed by the same laws throughout all time and space, for God is *Principle, law.* The laws governing man are laws of Love, creating and maintaining a home for him that is obedient to God's order, plan, and purpose for it. The universe and man are harmonious because the divine Principle, Love, is the only Law-maker and all laws operate to bless what they govern.

Spiritual man and the universe are one with this eternal Principle that includes not only the physical laws of the universe, but also the moral laws of the Scriptures, and the spiritual laws of divine Science. Law, order, plan, and purpose are as absolute in governing man as they are in governing the universe. In reality all substance, visible and invisible, is governed and maintained according to divine law. The law of love, the law of honesty, the law of intelligence, the law of purity, the law of harmony, the law of abundance — to name a few — are spiritual laws. These laws, designed to bless God's creation, are the *only* laws governing it.

The one divine Principle is available to everyone, everywhere, all the time. Like the principle of mathematics or music, the laws of God are ever present for us to draw upon as we come to understand them. We will come to think and live in these laws as effortlessly as we now think and live in scientific laws. They are the basis to our being, our world, our universe, and we will learn to obey them because they operate to bless us beyond measure.

The creativity and originality of God are described by the synonym, *Soul, identity*. Beauty, harmony, and perfection originate in Soul and are individualized in the creations of a dynamic universe. Soul images forth forms that reflect Godlike qualities. Soul is the source of the evolutionary changes that carry forth a dynamic creation.

The presence of design, found everywhere in everything, is not only practical, workable design, but it expresses artistic beauty and originality, charm and grace. These delightful qualities come from Soul. Not only does Soul create all things real, but it also makes them beautiful, individual, unique — worthy to be called God's handiwork. And since God creates through atomic action and form, there is no limit to His originality. From a handful of basic elements He creates great galaxies and fragile flowers, towering mountains and tiny snowflakes. Even though there is infinite diversity and originality in creation, all things conform to the law of harmony and perfection. Thus, the substance, form, and life of all things are divinely good. God is the Soul of the universe and man, the source of all individuality.

Man's own genius comes from the mind that discerns the creativity of Soul. When the inmost thoughts are freed of materialism and mortal emotions, they become a transparency for Soul's inspiration. Great originality takes place in a thought so spiritualized that it can discern the ideas of Soul. The one Mind unfolds original ideas as the human mind reaches out to the infinite. As we learn to recognize this Soul-filled realm of ideas as the source of our true identity, God's thoughts become our thoughts, and we find our true selfhood in His likeness.

When we reason on the subject of God in this way, the illusion of matter and animal magnetism fade out, and we recognize Spirit to be the real cause and source of our being. Here and now we are celestial ideas, not earth-bound creatures; but to understand this, we must press through the boundaries of the mind and take consciousness to a new level, where we *feel* the presence of the divine Principle, Love. Through the seven synonyms we learn to reason from a spiritual basis, and as we pray, God grows increasingly real to us, drawing us ever closer to the true source of our being. We see that God as cause and man as effect are inseparable here and now.

We seem to have a body that is material. We seem to live in a world of material cause and effect. But we transcend this view as we look through the visible, tangible forms and acknowledge beneath them a spiritual cause, invisible but ever present.

Second Footstep: Relating Man to the Synonyms

In our prayerful work, we should relate the synonyms to man. A spiritual cause would not create a material man in a material universe, nor would it create a spiritual man and put him in a material universe. So man and the universe must be spiritual. The more clearly we see ourselves and our world as spiritual ideas embodying spiritual qualities and governed by divine laws, the happier our lives. To realize this, we can relate man to the synonyms, and realize that *we are that man.*

Man is spiritual. Being created by a spiritual cause, formed by the thoughts of God, his form must ultimately be seen as a "thought-form" governed by the thoughts and feelings that reflect *Spirit* alone. The substance of Spirit comprises man's being. He lives in a harmless body and a perfect universe. Because all things are designed to provide a perfect home for man, God would not put in it a single harmful element. All things real exist to bless and prosper him. Man is not a mortal form in a material universe, but spiritual entity in a heavenly home, one with God.

Because man has life, he must be an expression of *Life* and embody all the qualities of Life. He is one with God, his true Father-Mother, in the "eternal now." Created in God's likeness, he reflects the same qualities that are found in God. Expressing the substance of Life, his body cannot be weary or sick or aged. He has inexhaustible energy, perfect health, and the joy of knowing that he is immortal. Nothing can come between him and the Father, for there is nothing greater than God. God is All-in-all, and embraces His idea, man, in harmony and perfection throughout eternity. If there is no matter in reality, then there is nothing to be sick or die, nothing to wear out or grow old.

The man of God's making is eternal. His life is indestructible. As we learn this, the fear of disease and death lifts. Our immortality is linked to God's eternal presence. We learn to live in the "eternal now." As we identify with the Life that is all good, and reject material theories, we begin to live in the spiritual dimension. Knowing this to some degree has a very positive effect on health, longevity, and endurance.

Truth is the Science of man's being. He knows God is All, and he knows he knows. He is beyond illusions because he cannot have both Truth and error in the same mind at the same time.

It is very reassuring to know that God is Truth. As we understand the spiritual realm, we arrive at Truth, for there is nothing beyond God, nor are there many gods, many causes — only one cause creating one universe and man. What we know and prove concerning God is forever. Man's entire being is established on the rock of Truth. The Science of God manifests in man a life that is complete, secure, safe. This Science is eternal. It never changes, and so man rests secure in knowing that Truth will always be present as the substance of his being.

To understand this Truth is to be free of the illusion of matter and animal magnetism. It is to arrive at the true Science, and there is great peace in proportion as Truth becomes real to us.

Man, as the expression of *Love*, is loving, gentle, kind, compassionate, forgiving, patient, humble, and generous. His nature is the embodiment of Christ-like qualities, which he expresses effortlessly, because love is his true nature in God's image. Man lives in an environment filled with God's lovingkindness. In this atmosphere of Love, he is inseparable from his true Father and Mother. And he reflects divine Love in a heart and soul and mind that is as pure in goodness as Love itself.

Divine Love goes much deeper than human affection. Love permeates all that is real. It is what God *feels* for us. It is the motive behind all that He does for us.

It is comforting to know that the substance of all being is Love. Because God is Love, He could not create a substance that is harmful, hard, cold, painful, capable of inflicting suffering on His idea, man.

Love opens the door to deeper insights into God's nature, for it dissolves the beliefs and emotions of a materialistic mind, and softens the inner self so that it is receptive to God's ideas. Love as taught in the Sermon on the Mount is essential in order to plumb the depths of the hidden realm and understand it.

Man lives in an inexhaustible reservoir of ideas of the one *Mind*. Listening from within, he never lacks for intelligence, wisdom, and understanding in all that relates to his experience. By understanding this Mind, he thinks at one with it for it is the substance of his being. The intelligence of Mind is so absolute and ever present that there is no place or time in which any other mind can exist. Man draws his entire being from the one Mind, and the ideas of Mind, unfolding as his being, take form in happiness, health, beauty, and goodness. Having an infinite reservoir of ideas to draw upon, he can never experience lack.

The ideas of Mind appear to us as we need and can understand them. As we expand our thought to see the presence of Mind as our Mind, this source of infinite ideas becomes ours to use in inspiring, creative, intelligent, and practical ways.

Because the one *Principle* governs man, he lives in a universe governed by spiritual laws that operate to bless him in every way. With his life anchored in Principle, man knows that the substance of his being can never be separated from the law, order, unity, plan and purpose that God has ordained for him.

Principle is a synonym that gives a sense of security and continuity to our life and our world. When our inmost thoughts rest in God as Principle, we know there is an unchanging foundation beneath us. Scientific, moral, and spiritual laws are absolute in this foundation, and mental obedience to them brings health and happiness.

The synonym *Soul* originates the identity of each idea that God expresses, and gives to each idea an individuality uniquely its own. Man's individuality is an expression of God's grace and beauty. Soul bestows on man everything desirable for a joyous life — beauty, grace, creativity, individuality, charm, poise, warmth, and humor. Each idea is an expression of the Soul-like qualities of the one Father-Mother God.

As an expression of Soul, man embodies the qualities of Soul. He rejoices that his life and his world are one of original ideas, each expressing the substance of Soul. According to the law of individuality, each must express his identity uniquely, yet always in a way that reflects God.

As we think about this realm as the source of our being and identify with it, we begin to experience our true selfhood and real life, for it is the truth about our being as God's idea.

Through this prayerful analysis of God and man, we become conscious of the presence of this realm. Such visionary ideas may seem idealistic, but time will reveal that they are true. The more we understand God through the synonyms and realize that man is made in His likeness, the easier it is to draw upon the healing power in the spiritual realm.

Third Footstep: Denying the Reality of Matter, Mortal Mind, and Animal Magnetism

These two subjects — God and man — are the affirmative part of our daily study and prayerful work. As we become familiar with the synonyms and the affirmation part of treatment, we are able to counteract the mesmerism of matter, mortal mind, and animal magnetism.

Studying the synonyms and affirming them in prayerful work is not enough to rid consciousness of all mesmerism. To be successful in our healing work, we need to know what animal magnetism is, how it operates, and how scientific prayer can free us of it.

Therefore, having affirmed God and man through the synonyms, the third step is to deny the reality of matter, mortal mind, and animal magnetism. In the denial part of treatment, we face the illusion of matter, mortal mind, and evil, and vehemently deny their reality or power. We need to take the initiative and aggressively reject every false impression relating to them.

As we understand God as All-in-all, we can make this denial with the growing conviction that God is real and they are unreal. Detecting and rejecting an illusion is not complicated. It is done with the synonyms in a direct and simple way. For example, consider the following analysis of matter:

If matter is an illusion, is there any spirituality in it? Is it a divine idea, originating in the one Mind? Is there any intelligence or wisdom in an illusion? Does it have a mind that can think? Is it the truth about man and the universe? Can an illusion be a scientific fact? Does an illusion have any feeling of love? Can it create a harmless environment for man? Does mindless matter have life? Can it create a living thing, or give plan and direction to evolution? Is it the origin of law, plan, order, and purpose in the universe? Is it based on a principle? Do material laws and causes have the intelligence or creativity to turn a few basic elements into the infinite originality, beauty, and harmony of a universe such as the one we know? Is there a soul in godless material forms? Of course not!

Matter cannot think or feel. It cannot create living creatures of such infinite complexity as we have found them to be. Matter cannot intelligently order or plan or direct the continuous evolution of the universe as we are coming to know it. Therefore, the denial of matter clears away the mist so that the light of Truth can reach us.

We can most effectively deny matter through the synonyms. Think carefully about your denials as you make them:

There is no spirit or substance in matter, and no matter in *Spirit*. Substance has no more solid substance than a thought or a feeling. It is a harmless medium that God images forth. All cause and effect is a closed spiritual system, void of matter and its so-called laws.

There is no life or being in matter, and no matter in *Life*. Life, God, is not dependent on any material law, cause or effect in creating and maintaining the universe and man. Life is not lived in a material medium

There is no mind or intelligence in matter, and no matter in *Mind*. The intelligence of the one Mind is never contaminated by the false belief in a cause or substance apart from God. Matter is unknown to Mind because they are complete opposites. The darkness of belief in matter cannot exist in the pure light of divine intelligence.

There is no truth or reality in matter, and no matter in *Truth*. Divine Science explains reality as originating in God, and this Science is the Truth that destroys the belief in material law, cause and effect.

There is no love or power in matter, and no matter in *Love*. The gentle love and tender care of the one Father-Mother, God, does not encase man in a form that could harm or destroy him. Man lives and moves and has his being in an atmosphere of pure Love void of all matter.

There is no principle or law in matter, and no matter in *Principle*. The laws of Principle, which operate to bless man, fill all time and space, making null and void any claim of matter and its laws.

There is no soul or substance in matter, and no matter in *Soul*. All identity and individuality are the expression of Soul, and are purely Godlike, void of any element that would harm or deform it mentally or physically.

Next we need to aggressively deny the mortal mind that believes in matter and evil as real.

The belief in matter is the cause of negative traits that must be detected and rejected through the treatment. This part of our work is personal, for we each have a different combination of traits, due to our individual personalities. But these traits can usually be traced to a few basic emotions — fear, self-will, and hatred. In this part of the treatment we need to analyze the negative traits that make up our human personality and determine those that need to be overcome in order to be a transparency for God's thoughts.

Many false characteristics of hatred, fear, and self-will are present in our inmost thoughts. Jealousy, envy, criticism, anger, timidity, anxiety, self-condemnation, domination, manipulation, deceit, dishonesty, injustice, malice, revenge, and many more mortal traits make up mortal selfhood. We need to handle such forms of animal magnetism in our treatment as we detect them and see that they are foreign to our Godlike nature.

Careful analysis will reveal how much of our mortal personality is formed from fear of lack, disease, adversity, age, etc., which is also accompanied by the belief that matter is the medium we live in. By denying matter, we can then detect and reject mortal emotions that stem from our belief in it.

We can begin this part of the treatment by handling *fear*. If the very foundation of being is Life, Truth, Love, then there is nothing to fear. God is All-in-all, so there is nothing outside of Him to fear. He is Love, so there is nothing in God to fear, nor can we be afraid of God, for He can only bless His creation and man. In the whole of creation, there is no harmful element, no poisonous atmosphere, no destructive force to fear.

Then we can know there is nothing to *hate* since Love blesses each idea impartially, bestowing unlimited good on all. There is no criticism, jealousy, envy, hostility, or anger in God's universe. All ideas dwell together in harmony and love, for each draws on the one God for his every need.

As the expression of God, man humbly obeys God's will, knowing that the divine will blesses him, whereas *self-will* acts contrary to his own good and produces the negative energy that brings pain and suffering. Man's only desire is to do God's will.

Careful thought needs to be given to the mortal emotions that accompany the belief in matter, for these emit destructive energy. We need to detect them and deny them as forms of animal magnetism in order to be free of them. We overcome them when we see that they are foreign to our Godlike nature and need to be denied. As we replace the belief in matter with the understanding that all substance is of God, these negative emotions lessen and disappear. But it is usually necessary to detect and reject many of them specifically, for they make up our mortal personality and need to be handled as animal magnetism.

We come now to the last crucial part of the treatment — *handling animal magnetism.* Here the recognition of God's all-ness is used to break down evil's seeming power and reality. Spiritual reasoning shows that God is the only cause, and that energy and form come from the ideas or thoughts emanating from Him. Harmless substance comprises all that He creates and maintains. However, matter and mortal mind seem to have a hidden cause or source — *animal magnetism.* While God is the real cause, animal magnetism also seems to be a cause imaging forth a material universe and mortal man. Although God alone is real, animal magnetism is an illusion so strong in consciousness that we cannot write it off as "nothing." It is an unseen hypnotic force that sometimes seems to be a power greater than God. Just as God is an unseen spiritual force, animal magnetism appears to be an unseen hypnotic evil force. Actually it is a form of *universal hypnotism* so deeply entrenched in individual and world consciousness that we cannot ignore it. We must face it and wrestle with its seeming power and reality until we overcome its mesmeric hold on us.

We begin this work by separating reality, with its positive thoughts and feelings, from the illusion of animal magnetism, with its negative emotions and beliefs. Having realized the allness of God, and having rejected matter and mortality, we then face the belief in evil and deny that it has power or reality.

It is essential to handle unseen evil as the underlying cause of matter and mortal existence. If we limit our work to denying the belief in matter, the work is incomplete. We need to look through the visible forms and deny the unseen cause of matter in order to be free of all illusion in matter and its laws.

Having realized the Truth about God and man, we can now bring this powerful Truth to bear on the illusion that animal magnetism is real. As we do this, we begin to be free of its hypnotic influence. This is possible because its influence has no reality or power to enforce its claims. *Evil is hypnotism. Mortal mind is hypnotism. Matter is hypnotism.* By striking at the unseen source, we destroy its seeming power. In denying matter, we reject the visible or tangible form of evil. But in denying animal magnetism, we reject the invisible cause or origin of the belief in matter and mortality.

This denial involves recognizing this unseen hypnotic force and declaring that there is no law, power, intelligence, substance or reality in it. There is no God in evil, and no evil in God. There is no life, or being in evil and no evil in Life; no truth or reality in evil ,and no evil in Truth; no love or power in evil, and no evil in Love; no mind or intelligence in evil, and no evil in Mind; no spirit or substance in evil, and no evil in Spirit; no soul or identity in evil, and no evil in Soul; no principle or law in evil, and no evil in Principle. Then, because it is hypnotic illusion, you can demand that it stop mesmerizing or influencing you. Declare, as Christ Jesus did, "You are a liar and the father of it." In this part of the treatment, you take a strong stand and vehemently deny that animal magnetism has any power to hypnotize or influence you.

This strong denial can bring about a noticeable change in consciousness. There are some beliefs of animal magnetism that cannot be overcome in any way other than by specifically arguing against them until they actually weaken and disappear from consciousness. Such prayerful work can free the mind of the false belief of matter and evil, and in place of the seeming vacuum, the divine reality unfolds, and the realm of God grows ever more real.

Final Footstep: Reestablishing the Oneness of God and Man

After denying matter, mortal mind, and animal magnetism, we should conclude the treatment by reaffirming the oneness of God and man so that the treatment does not end on a negative note. Lift thought into an inspired sense of the oneness of God as the

Father and Mother of man, and man as His perfect child. God is cause and man is effect — a relationship that is indestructible throughout eternity.

Summary

To summarize the most effective method of understanding the hidden realm of Mind:

First, it requires a dedication to the study of Christian Science found in Mrs. Eddy's writings and other advanced literature on Christian Science, and of course, dedicated study of the spiritual truths found in the Bible. This study is an education in divine metaphysics. This free form of prayer is essential to transforming consciousness. It will bring about definite changes in how you think.

Second, you need to learn how to give a good Christian Science treatment. This form of scientific prayer has four main footsteps: Affirming God through the synonyms; affirming man through the synonyms; denying the reality of matter, mortal mind, and animal magnetism; reaffirming the oneness of God and man in His likeness.

As we study and pray in this way, we find new ideas appearing in consciousness, opening up for us this hidden realm of Mind. These ideas spiritualize consciousness as the true view replaces the false, material view, and transforms the inner self. Our prayers become deeply inspired with the presence of God. This new state of mind frees us of the mesmerism of matter and evil. We learn about this spiritual realm first through study, then through prayer. There is no other way to understand the healing power latent in this hidden realm. This prayer, moreover, has to be a *scientific prayer*, in which we affirm the truth about God and man, *and* deny the reality of matter and animal magnetism. As we work with the treatment, we learn to "pray without ceasing."

How do we know if this prayer is right? By its healing effects. When we pray, spiritual ideas overcome the mesmerism of animal magnetism. Then it is a law that this improved state of mind must move forth and manifest itself in health and happiness. The better our understanding of God, the less suffering and discord we experience. When our consciousness is filled with Truth and Love, with divine substance and intelligence, it is incapable of any harmful energy. Through this transcending state of mind, we leave behind the dark, discordant images of the false material view, and slowly emerge into the spiritual realm.

A RETURN TO FAITH

God shall wipe away all tears from their eyes; and there shall be no more death, neither sorrow, nor crying, neither shall there be any more pain, for the former things are passed away. And he that sat upon the throne said, Behold, I make all things new. And he said unto me, Write: for these words are true and faithful.

REVELATION 21:4

Take courage, dear reader, for any seeming mysticism surrounding realism is explained in the Scripture, "There went up a mist from the earth [matter];" and the mist of materialism will vanish as we approach spirituality, the realm of reality; cleanse our lives in Christ's righteousness; bathe in the baptism of Spirit, and awake in His likeness.

MARY BAKER EDDY

Chapter VIII

A RETURN TO FAITH

The time will come when the Theory of Everything will be revealed to a gifted mind, and we will know one more secret that lies hidden in the mysterious realm of the one Mind. This equation will shed more light on the mathematical precision of the universe, but it will not define the *whole* of Mind.

The major scientific fields are coming to recognize the realm beyond the senses. In the closing decades of the Twentieth Century, some scientists were predicting that the coming age would be one of metaphysics. At the same time, many Christian Scientists were beginning to outgrow a very regimented religious organization, to become the more accomplished metaphysicians that this Science requires, and to make better use of the infinite possibilities it offers.

In the past Christian Science ran counter to scientific views about God and man, but now this Science is in tune with the most advanced scientific theories. Those who study it are moving with the current of world thought, unlocking the secrets, and opening the door to the realm of God.

In the overall scheme of things, these small turning points may seem insignificant. Yet they indicate a change so dramatic and irreversible that they could someday be recognized as the most important events in the history of mankind. The merging of science and religion is not yet obvious, but science is leading us back to faith in God. And as we move ever deeper into this spiritual realm, science and religion will eventually become one. As natural science continues to acknowledge the hidden realm of Mind, Christian Science will continue moving towards its destiny as the key to it.

The anthropic principle will grow stronger as we continue

to discover the harmony and perfection of God's handiwork, and our image of the universe evolves into something closer to the ultimate Truth. It is impossible to change a material universe into a spiritual one, but we can change our mental image of it from matter to Spirit. We can change how we think; that is all we need to do.

Can we understand this realm beyond the senses? That we are endowed with the ability to do so has already been proven in the Christian Science movement, for its history is filled with a record of healings that have come from an understanding of the spiritual nature of man in God's likeness. Thousands upon thousands of testimonies are found in Christian Science periodicals, books, and lectures, and these represent only the smallest fraction of the healings that have taken place — most of them never recorded. This Science has blessed people in all walks of life. This is proof that the world is filled with minds capable of understanding Christian Science and demonstrating its healing power.

This healing work is the result of individual prayer, and is evidence that healing and regeneration are possible to everyone, everywhere, at any time. Those who want to learn about this realm can pray their way into it and become accomplished in spiritual healing. Simply introducing spiritual ideas into consciousness begins to de-mesmerize it, piercing the darkness of materialism with spiritual enlightenment and opening the door to freedom from material laws that seem to imprison us.

One thing that we need in order to experience such freedom is *faith* — faith in God as the Supreme Being, and faith in our ability to understand Him. We cannot create in our own minds a form of intelligence we have never known. We must pray for it, and we must have faith that God will give it to us. This receptivity to God's thoughts transforms consciousness. We come to discern His thoughts and feel His presence with us.

When Mrs. Eddy realized that she had discovered the scientific laws underlying Christ Jesus' healing works, she recorded it in her textbook, *Science and Health with Key to the Scriptures*.

This book became the foundation of her Cause. Other religions have various forms of literature, but none *began* with a textbook as complete and powerful as *Science and Health*. It is unique to Christian Science.

From the time Mrs. Eddy's book was first published, many were healed by reading it, and they became ardent Christian Scientists. Time has not dimmed the devotion of those students who recognize what she has given the world. It is hard to describe the loyalty and gratitude Scientists feel for Mrs. Eddy. They have been saved from suffering and pain, invalidism and death, poverty and grief through her writings. Christian Science has changed their views of God and Satan, Spirit and matter, life and death.

It is an unforgettable experience to feel the darkness closing in, to be suffering from an incurable or terminal disease, to be in the depths of grief or loneliness, to know only lack and limitation, and then find God's help and healing though Christian Science.

This Science is far more than a creed one subscribes to. It is a very advanced scientific discovery requiring a progressive education in divine metaphysics. Mrs. Eddy's Church was basically an educational institution. It included Bible Lesson-Sermons for the daily study of the Bible and *Science and Health*. *The Christian Science Journal* and *Christian Science Sentinel* published metaphysical articles, testimonies of healing, and listed Christian Science practitioners and teachers worldwide. The Church began to educate its members in a revelation that heals even the most hopeless illness and meets the most desperate human needs.

Christian Scientists of the Twentieth Century were mainly devoted to serving the Church. Their practice of Christian Science was more one of faith and unquestioning loyalty to the Church. They relied on practitioners for healing, because these dedicated workers had phenomenal healing results. Mrs. Eddy had many students who became practitioners and teachers. They understood how to pray and find healing, and they taught their own students this healing art. But this spirituality, so strong in the early years of the Church, has slowly diminished because the Church is gradually going the way of all religious organizations. It has so diluted its presentation of Christian Science that the Science as Mrs. Eddy taught it, is rapidly disappearing within the formal organization.

But as this decline takes place within the Church, there is coming forth new life independent of the organization. Today we have something the early Scientists did not have — a vast collection of writings by some of the finest Christian Scientists of the past. It includes the unpublished writings of Mrs. Eddy, the memoirs and metaphysical papers of her students, teachers' addresses to their association of students, articles and lectures by some of the finest Christian Scientists in the movement, and books published independently of the Church. This inspired literature, studied in conjunction with the Bible and Mrs. Eddy's published writings, is taking Christian Science to a new level — one beyond the Church into a universal study in which the individual understands how to demonstrate its healing power. This progressive step is already taking place within the movement. With so many excellent books and papers available, many Scientists are devoting themselves to a deeper study of this Science. They are finding that prayer in Christian Science is as effective today as it has ever been.

These Scientists are the *avant-garde* of the Spiritual Age. They are the remnant of the Christian Science movement. Will the world follow their example and press into this hidden realm, or will the growing evil that is gathering temporarily put out the light shining in the darkness? As the challenges of today grow, the future hangs in the balance.

Over six thousand years ago civilization began. Men still are at war. Sickness and disease are common place. Crime and terrorism are an ever-present threat. Witchcraft and mind-control are being practiced by people of all ages. Our only refuge and escape from these latter days and the only answer to these challenges, is in the spiritual realm, where God gives us protection from danger, heals our sickness and disease, and unfolds answers to the problems beyond the reach of science and technology.

It would be encouraging to think that a beautiful equation — a Theory of Everything — could enable us to "know the Mind of God." Unfortunately, it is not going to be that easy. The universal remedy for the woes of mankind is hidden in the spiritual realm, waiting for us to think and pray our way into it. Everything we need to begin this grand adventure of the mind has been provided.

Beyond the senses there lies this infinite Mind that has designed the cell and calculated the force of gravity to 10^{-40}. Is it a coincidence that the discovery of a supreme intelligence underlying the universe and the revelation of Christian Science should appear at the same time in the history of civilization?

I don't think so. . . .

Bibliographical References

Behe, Michael J., *Darwin's Black Box*,
    The Free Press, New York, 1996
Boslough, John, *Masters of Time*,
    Addison-Wesley Publishing Co., 1992
Brockelman, Paul, *Cosmology and Creation*,
    Oxford University Press, New York, 1999
Clark, Robert E. D., *The Universe: Plan or Accident?*
    Muhlenberg Press, 1961
Crick, Francis, *Life Itself, Its Origin and Nature*,
    Simon and Schuster, 1981
Darling, David, *Equations of Eternity*, Hyperion, 1993
Davies, Paul, *The Mind of God*, Simon and Schuster, 1992
Davies, Paul and Gribbin, John, *The Matter Myth*,
    Simon and Schuster, 1992
Denton, Michael J., *Nature's Destiny*, The Free Press, 1998
Ferguson, Kitty, *The Fire in the Equations*,
    William B. Eerdmans Publishing Co. 1994
Glynn, Patrick, *God: The Evidence*, Prima Publishing, 1997
Greene, Brian, *The Elegant Universe*,
    W. W. Norton and Co., 1999
Hawking, Stephen W., *A Brief History of Time*,
    Bantam Books, 1988
Horgan, John, *The End of Science*, Helix Books, 1995
Jastrow, Robert, *The Enchanted Loom*,
    Simon and Schuster, 1981
Lederman, Leon, *The God Particle*, Houghton Mifflin Co., 1993
Lerner, Eric J., *The Big Bang Never Happened*,
    Simon and Schuster, 1991
McTaggart, Lynne, *The Field*, Harper Collins Publishers, 2002
Penrose, Roger, *The Emperor's New Mind*,
    Oxford University Press, 1989
Schroeder, Gerald L., *The Hidden Face of God*,
    The Free Press, 2001
    The Science of God, The Free Press, 1997
Stewart, Ian, *Nature's Numbers*, Basic Books, 1995

ABOUT THE AUTHOR: Ann Beals is a life-long Christian Scientist. Her family came into Christian Science through a healing she had before she was a year old. Doctors could not diagnose the illness or cure it. She seemed about to pass on when her mother called in a Christian Science practitioner who prayed for her until she regained consciousness. Within a short time she was completely healed. Her parents then took up the study of Christian Science and the family attended First Church of Christ, Scientist in Louisville, Kentucky. During her early years she had several healings of extremely serious illnesses through reliance on Christian Science. In time her father, Harry Smith, became a Christian Science teacher and lecturer.

While attending Washington University in St. Louis, Missouri, Ms. Beals met and married Robert Beals. She has two sons, Charles and John. After serving the branch church in Decatur, Georgia, in many ways, she became a Christian Science practitioner, listed in *The Christian Science Journal*. She also contributed a number of articles to the Christian Science periodicals.

Early in her practice work, she realized the need for writings that explained more fully how to demonstrate Christian Science. But when she submitted deeper articles to the editors of the periodicals, they were unwilling to publish them.

As she watched the steady decline of the Christian Science Church, her concern for the future of the movement led her, in 1974, to publish independently of the Church organization her booklet *Animal Magnetism*. Because of Church policy, members of the Church, and especially *Journal* listed practitioners, were forbidden to publish writings without the permission of the Christian Science Board of Directors. After publishing her booklet, she was forced to resign her *Journal* listing as a practitioner.

In 1975, she met Reginald G. Kerry. He shared her deep concern about the decline in the Church. His work at Church headquarters in Boston had led him to see that the decline in the Church was largely due to the immorality and corruption at Church headquarters. He delivered an ultimatum to the Board of Directors that they either "clean up things at headquarters" or he would write Church members exposing the corruption and immorality there. When the Board refused to take his threat seriously, he carried out his promise to "write the field." Ms. Beals assisted him in sending the Kerry Letters. For two years, while living in Boston, she worked with him in getting out the first four Kerry Letters. Her book, *Crisis in the Christian Science Church*, tells of these events.

After mailing the fourth Kerry Letter, she moved to California. She resigned from the Church in 1977. She continued assisting the Kerrys in sending out the Letters. In 1980, she started The Bookmark with the conviction that the time had come when deeper writings on Christian Science had to be published and made available to everyone. As this work has progressed, she has been able to publish and promote many profound works on Christian Science that have been suppressed by the Board of Directors over the years.

She presently lives in Santa Clarita, California, where she continues to write papers on Christian Science, and serve as publisher and editor of The Bookmark.

For further information regarding Christian Science:
Write: The Bookmark
        Post Office Box 801143
        Santa Clarita, CA 91380
Call: 1-800-220-7767
Visit our website: www. thebookmark.com